Endorsement for
Spirit Winds with Chimes

How can you not love Daniel Dowidat? Poetry is the
language of the soul; and this is a man for whom the bril-
liance of sun and star, along with the darkness of storm and
sorrow, equally praise the name of God. This is a man
whose soul gives thanks through his poetry, and in that offering, blesses the Name.

Lotis Key
Christian novelist:*The Song of the Tree, A Thing Devoted*
Director / Producer (www.themessengersfeet.org)
Seminar speaker on Writing for Christian Theater
Vice President - Minnesota Christian Writers Guild

SPIRIT WINDS

WITH
CHIMES

By Daniel P. Dowidat

Spirit Winds with Chimes
Copyright © 2013 by Daniel P. Dowidat

Published by TrueNorth Publishing,
6901 Ives Ln. N., Maple Grove, MN 55369
www.truenorthpublishingdt.com
Manufactured by Book Printing Revolution, Minneapolis, MN 55401

Unless otherwise noted, scriptures are taken from New American
Standard Bible (NASB), copyright 1960, 1963, 1968, 1971, 1972,
1973, 1975, 1977, by The Lockman Foundation. Used by permission.
All rights reserved.

Cover design, interior art, and layout: Cheryl Barr
Editing: Delores E. Topliff, Creative Design Services,
www.delorestopliff.com

ISBN 978-0-9842291-5-4

Published in the United States of America

Spirit Winds with Chimes, my second book, is lovingly dedicated to my wife, Lorayne June Dowidat, for her patiently hearing these poems, even when in primitive form. Her input as my Christ-given better half is invaluable. The subsection, "A Good Wife," poems grew from my love, knowledge and understanding of my good wife, her daily works and ways, including lasting appreciation for her many gifts and sweet companionship.

CONTENTS

SPIRIT WINDS

CHIMES

FOREWORD

When boys and girls, men and women, find personal faith in Christ, discovering their place in God's family makes it natural for them to praise Him. Some do that through song, some through words, and some through original specially crafted words—poetic expressions like the Bible's King David.

Daniel Dowidat, the author of *Spirit Winds with Chimes*, has that similar kind of close relationship with God. Like David, the sweet singer Psalmist of Israel, Dowidat is an intentional poet, a philosopher asking challenging questions as poems begin and exploring and answering most of them by each poem's end. Within this volume he considers most topics under the sun. You are warmly invited to spend minutes or hours reading poetic searchings and expressions that also may cause your heart to soar. Or Dowidat's inspired words may lead you to resolve deep-heart matters or provide the understanding needed to let go of issues that until now have prevented healing and freedom.

Come enter these pages. Share the beauty, profound considerations, and conclusions that are all hallmarks of Dowidat's own journey.

Delores E. Topliff,
Author and President, Minnesota Christian Writers Guild
Adjunct Professor, Northwestern College, St. Paul, Minnesota
www.delorestopliff.com

The heart of these poems springs from my love for God's Word along with the observations and perceptions of a lifetime. My key Scripture is Matthew 12:34 (KJV). Jesus said, "…for out of the abundance of the heart the mouth speaketh." Over the years I have nourished my heart with the glories of God through studying scripture and His creation. Its sights, sounds, scents, and touch trigger my senses producing the enclosed spiritual and poetic responses that are gifts from God. I'm continually astounded by God's revelations in these pages. They draw me at times out of despair or frustration into hope and joy. My sincere desire is that you too will be refreshed and know more of the hope and joy I have found while creating *Spirit Winds with Chimes*.

Daniel P. Dowidat – Minneapolis 2013

INTRODUCTION

"Write what you know." "Write what you like to read." Both statements are helpful directives for hopeful writers; wise parameters which if followed should lead to success.

Yet we all fall short in conveying God's glory. For me, writing what I know has its roots in God's Scriptures. Though I have a master's degree from only one seminary, my Christian education extends before and after this educational experience into many classrooms in other colleges and seminars attended. I have the experience of being raised in a Christian family knowing God's words and ways. I earned a bachelor's degree in Forestry from the University of Minnesota and a master's degree in Theological Studies from Bethel Seminary, St. Paul.

My life studies in God's creation led me to the career in Forestry. It began through my deep love for God's great outdoors experienced through hiking, fishing, hunting, camping, studying animal lore and plant agronomy as a youth. For the past thirty years my training intensified as I took advantage of opportunities to study God's word in depth in churches, colleges, universities, and seminaries. These educational pursuits were accomplished while experiencing the wonders of God's creation while working as a forester. This combined background birthed the poems in this book. What we put into our lives, these earthen vessels created by God, determines what comes out. Our common humanity makes none of us exempt to fears, trials and tribulations, but we can also experience the joys and hopes birthed in our hearts by our loving

Creator. *Spirit Winds with Chimes* expresses the hopes God has written in my heart.

The second writing directive is "Write what you like to read." During the past thirty years I've been intensely involved in serious Bible study. My list of influences and involvements is long. Accomplishing it all has taken Research! Research! Research! I read reference books by the droves on any subject currently involved in. For that reason *Spirit Winds with Chimes* is fashioned like a poetic reference book of biblical knowledge and beauty, numbered 1-150. Poems are categorized relating to the beauties found in nature as well as to the complex lives of humans, experiencing trials with truths gained.

This book contains two groups of 75 poems each. The first half, *Spirit Winds*, reflects on the character of the Godhead with primary emphasis on natural creation. The second half, *Chimes*, presents 75 additional poems considering the emotions and experiences common to mankind as we journey life and glean. I hope this categorization makes it easy to use these poems regarding trials or happiness experienced in readers' lives. Do you have a joy to share? Find a category with a suitable message to fit your life situation. Do you need to be lifted from the doldrums? These poems result from wisdom found in God's hope book, the Bible. May every poem carry His fragrance of hope, no matter your circumstance. May their spiritual truths cleanse and refresh you in body, mind and spirit.

SPIRIT WINDS

THE SOURCE

The Godhead

1 Spirit Winds

When fears and doubts creep in and crouch,
As enemies to our soul,
Then look to Him who stills the wind,
That blows us out of control.

The words of God above this sod,
Calm our hearts and souls,
Bringing love to all mankind,
Comforting lives down here below.

Each soul of man is in God's plan,
Tendered by self-control.
Disciplines of mind are gifts of Thine,
To the sons and daughters You know.

Restore our hearts lest fears and doubts,
Waft us beyond control.
The heart of man rests in Your hands,
As Spirit Winds gently blow.

John 3:8 *Jesus said, "The wind blows where it wishes and you hear the sound of it, but do not know where it comes from and where it is going; so is everyone who is born of the Spirit."*

2 Honor the Father

Our Father who art in heaven,
We worship You today.
We sing to you with thankful hearts,
For all the lives you save.

Men of honor lift this song,
Upholding You in praise.
Men devoted to life so strong,
By the duty they display.

All the men who worship You,
Have longed to see Your day.
To you alone is honor due,
From those who kneel and pray.

Father of all whom You created,
Live through us today.
Man's worth on earth is reinstated,
As we walk Your holy ways.

Matthew 5:48 *Therefore you are to be perfect, as your heavenly Father is perfect.*

3 Honor the Son

Creating lives in the heart of God,
His mysteries to perform.
He entrusts to man this land we've trod,
Guided by principles of His reform.

When guided by our God above,
Each one is tendered by His love.
We have a God who understands,
Reaching out with nail pierced hands.

This planet earth He onetime trod,
He lived with us here in flesh and blood.
Are we so blind that we don't see,
His love extends from sea to sea?

God's gifts of food supply the flesh,
Renewing the soul within us blessed.
Clothing and shelter we take for granted,
Though they're gifts of love by God extended.

We look around at those in need,
While our own lives may expose greed.
But guided in God's ways by love,
Our lives project His heavens above.

His love shines forth within each life,
When we become a living sacrifice.
Our lives are then sacrificed for others,
By selfless giving to our brothers.

This world created for God the Son,
Reveals His mysteries have just begun.
Our lives when lived in Christ as one,
Reveal to all what God has done.

Colossians 1:16 *For by Him (the Christ) all things were created, both in the heavens and on earth, visible and invisible, whether thrones or dominions or rulers or authorities—all things have been created through Him and for Him.*

4 For me to live is Christ

For me to live is Christ rings within my heart,
In this world God's hand gives us a new start.
Forgiveness is the key to life,
Bringing freedom from inner strife.

Forgiven, forgotten, words we love to hear,
Originates from the God we love and fear.
When guided by His principles above,
We are taught to fear and love.

Love is a blessing we temporally hold,
To give to others as we are told.
The gift of love is not ours to maintain,
But comes from God without constraint.

When love is given to us so bold,
God's grace to the masses begins to unfold.
Love is a gift that all of us cherish,
It is Gods desire that none of us perish.

For this cause we turn from our sin,
Embracing Gods love emanating within.
Repentant lives within God's hands,
Return changed hearts to God and man.

John 15:5 *Jesus said, "I am the vine, you are the branches; he who abides in Me and I in him, he bears much fruit, for apart from Me you can do nothing."*

5 Heartfelt

Love abounds when in Christ we're found,
His life He gives that we may live.
When in this world troubles surround,
Turn to God who gently forgives.

The love of God tenderly provides,
Gifts necessary for each to survive.
When in doubt don't turn aside,
For our sins Christ was crucified.

If He died for me, why don't I see,
To save my life it had to be?
When in our hearts He lives to stay,
We'll rise triumphant another day.

We'll rise in love above the skies,
When for His glory we live His story.
Written on our hearts His message flies,
When our Creator returns to glory.

2 Corinthians 3:2–3 *You are our letter, written in our hearts, known and read by all men;.. written not with ink but with the Spirit of the living God....*

6 Wisdom Falling

When wise in each other's eyes,
Look to Him who was crucified.
Though worldly wisdom may be a bane,
To those of this world poor and lame.

Poor and lame in heart and mind,
Though once created for eternal times.
In Christ alone we do see,
Wisdom leading eternally.

It's Christ who died that we may live,
Above the tumult this world gives.
Destined to reign with Him above,
With Father, Son and Spirit in love.

Wisdom's river flows from Christ's throne,
Watering the gardens of life He's sown.
Causing every living thing to grow,
As beautiful and pure as new-fallen snow.

James 3:17 *But the wisdom from above is first pure, then peaceable, gentle, reasonable, full of mercy and good fruits, unwavering, without hypocrisy.*

7 Day and Night

A day and night can be a delight,
When lived in the light of God's glory.
How is this done? Look to His Son,
Into His life for the old, old story.

Where is this found? You were not around,
When angels encamped all around Him.
At Bethlehem He was found, a babe on this ground,
Heralded by angels and shepherds adoring Him.

What was His end? From Golgotha He began,
His new life to reign within us.
How is this done? Through the life of the Son,
In us He lives and sustains us.

How to begin? First look to our sin,
Until forgiven, forgotten forever.
Sins cast in the deep so we can now sleep,
Held in His life light as a feather.

Matthew 11:28–30 *Jesus said, "Come to Me, all*
who are weary and heavy-laden, and I will give you rest ..."

8 Christ Minded

Temptations, troubles and snares,
Mountains of earthly cares,
Abound before we strive,
For acceptance in God's eyes.

Though the earth may quake,
And heavens even shake,
Before Your throne of grace,
Our knees do bend in haste.

Impoverished, my soul does find,
You are forever kind,
Touching this life of mine,
With love from depths divine.

The heavens declare,
Your glory beyond compare.
When we reach beyond the stars,
The mind of Christ is ours.

1 Corinthians 2:16 *But we have the mind of Christ.*
For who has known the mind of the Lord, that He
will instruct Him?

9 Forever Free

Tell me the old, old story,
That Jesus died for me.
Tell me of His glory,
When He made the blind to see.

Tell me again of Jesus life,
In the land of Galilee.
Rising above storms and strife,
Walking upon the sea.

Tell me of His acts of kindness,
While hanging upon the tree.
Healing us of our blindness,
Setting the whole world free.

Tell of the gift He gave,
New life for all to see.
Released from life's destined grave,
Reborn, forever free.

John 8:36 *So if the Son makes you free, you will be free indeed.*

10 Sonshine

Peace will reign when the Son shines again,
The Son will rise His world to begin.
Death cannot keep Him, it never really could,
He paid for our lives by God's own shed blood.

God in His Son has been here to stay,
His love abounds each and every day.
He's never far from all who call on His name,
He lives in our hearts and minds, forever the same.

The unchanging qualities of our Lord without end,
Remain forever the same, just as He first began.
Creator of this world, sun, moon and stars,
Living now among us, deep in each heart.

The change occurs gradually within each life,
When Christ resides within, freeing of strife.
Turmoil within, gone by His command,
Calmed by Him who stills seas at His holy command.

Psalms 122:8 *For the sake of my brothers and my friends, I will now say, "May peace be within you."*

11 Bread From Paradise

A half loaf of bread from paradise,
Is always food enough to suffice,
Hungering palates of the world,
As heavens gates are unfurled.

The gates are open, our God does bless,
All seeking His true righteousness.
God's love restores and opens doors,
For us to live in Christ who we adore.

Christ died long ago for the human race,
Leaving behind forgiveness by grace.
How do we obtain this bread of life,
Sequestered from heaven's paradise?

Start by asking forgiveness of sins,
Forgotten forever when God lives within.
The feast will then truly start,
When you receive a brand new heart.

A heart that yearns for new life so bold,
That could never be bought or sold.
The bread of life so freely given;
Christ's gift to man from God in heaven.

John 6:47–51 *Jesus said, "Truly, truly, I say to you, he who believes has eternal life. I am the bread of life ...*

The Word

12 Wide and Deep

Once again the sun does shine,
The clouds of night departed.
Wake up, young man, and thank your God,
The heavens are kind hearted.

Lift up your eyes unto the hills,
In all your daytime endeavors.
The King of Kings is ruler still,
He reigns on high forever.

The long night is over, the new earth beckons,
Our path is lit with God's word that quickens.
Guard our hearts as we go forth,
With the glow God's Son has given.

Yield to God's call men and women of faith,
His promises aren't shaken.
His word when hidden deep in our hearts,
Brings life wonders you thought forsaken.

God's word, the Bible, looms wide and deep,
Calling each emerging from sleep.
Bringing light and love for all mankind,
By His grace we learn His love divine.

True light begins as a warm glow,
When in your heart He renews your soul.
Restored again, are hearts once broken,
Renewed by the words God's Son has spoken.

Isaiah 42:3 *A bruised reed He will not break*
And a dimly burning wick He will not
extinguish; He will faithfully bring forth justice.

11

13 God's Light Dawning

Bright morning light does now excite,
Our hearts bound in gladness.
Beside my wife I do delight,
As dawn arises from dark nights.

As dawn breaks forth, I can perceive,
That truth in life lies in God's light.
His light dispels all fears conceived,
When those born blind their sight receive.

Though blinded from birth by original sin,
Mankind sees God's plans unfolding.
Hearts seared and scarred harsh and deep,
Are now healed at Jesus feet.

His Son did live a tortured life,
That the world could begin to see,
A new world arising from dark night,
Within God's glorious revealing sight.

The effects of sin within God's world,
Are forever revealed and broken,
By obedience to God's inerrant word,
Which through His Son was spoken.

John 8:12 *Then Jesus again spoke to them, saying, "I am
the Light of the world; he who follows Me will not walk in
the darkness, but will have the Light of life."*

14 Feathers and Swords

Some things are complimentary when observed by eyes within,
The feather of compassion, and the sharp sword to conquer sin.
The eagle feather in this house belongs to my wife,
The sword of God's word, in my hand, struggles for life.

The feather of compassion maintains God's peace,
The sword of the Spirit helps sin to be released.
The wrath of God resides when these two are out of control,
The spirit of men and women are freed when love enfolds.

God's love springs forth from man to wife,
When through God's word we are freed from strife.
The sword of His Spirit is now set free,
When the Bible is used faithfully.

A loving wife brings lives together,
With compassionate use of her eagle feather.
Love kept strong for family and friends,
Is dispensed from God's free love within.

The sword of the Spirit in a man's hand,
Brings restoration unto lost lands.
For God and Country we do stand,
Tall and straight, part of God's band.

Psalms 91:4 (KJV) *He shall cover thee with his feathers, and under his wings shalt thou trust: his truth shall be thy shield and buckler.*

15 Restoration of Unity

Joy in this land lies in God's hand,
When His words bind us together.
A command to one may not fit another,
We all should act as sisters and brothers.

God's word is truth when it's proclaimed,
At times may take on different names.
We are guided by His word alone,
He's the one who creates talking stones.

Through Christ alone our voices rise;
Honoring God before men's eyes.
He hears us as we praise His name,
By word and deed His name's proclaimed.

The beliefs of one supports another,
When His word is declared by sisters and brothers.
Before noon today may we all say?
"We are united again," with no delay.

John 13:34–35 *Jesus said, "A new
commandment I give to you, that you love one another....*

16 Truth in Love

Truth in love comes from the depths of soul,
From our God above who richly bestows.
Love in man is fleeting, I'm told,
Found in God's word, that story of old.

Love from heart to heart begins at home,
With spouse and kids not left forlorn.
Love is pulled from the depth of hearts,
Warmed by God's word as the best start.

Begin by showing how God loved you,
In bringing you His words of truth.
That His Son died and rose again,
To redeem my life once smothered by sin.

Forgiveness means to turn to You,
In faith and love from my life renewed.
It begins with just one act at a time,
Extended to us through His heart and mine.

1 John 4:19 *We love, because He first loved us.*

17 God's Word Out of Pocket

God's word is to be used,
His Bible is not for storage.
Carried in your pocket or purse,
Its glories can restore us.

When out of pocket, opened and read,
God's word has power to raise the dead.
The words of Christ bring strength and power,
Read on any day or hour.

So renew your strength as the eagles,
Walk and run with life renewed.
Conduct your life within God's light,
As His words are read by you.

Your life shines from within your heart,
What you put in decides what departs.
God's love shines forth when His words report,
The light from a life lived in His full support.

Psalms 119:105 *Your word is a lamp to my feet*
and a light to my path.

18 Good News

Good news at night is such a delight,
Pleasant dreams surround our bed.
Good news at dawn makes one strong,
Anticipating goodness approaching ahead.

Start each day in God's word you say?
Bring brightness to life in His glory?
The heavens declare His light is most fair,
When viewed through His old, old story.

15

When you open each page, look to the Sage,
That wrote books of God's word in the Bible,
The light of His words from heaven are heard,
With thundering light for revival.

God opens blind eyes of those who denied,
The light of His words and glory.
Blind eyes can now see, the glory to be,
As God's Son rules by the words of His Story.

Psalms 119:105 *Your word is a lamp to my feet and a light to my path.*

19 Peace is Elusive

God the Son will hold us firm,
His eternal lessons we must learn.
We extinguish fires of strife every day,
When we bow our knees to Him and pray.

Peace on earth is not ours to make,
It is in God's love that He creates.
Peace to mankind is elusive,
When to our God we are abusive.

Obeying is for every nation and tongue,
God's peace will reign when this is done.
For His glory God wants to see,
Obedience by man to all His decrees.

His commands are for us behold,
Etched on stone and hearts, I'm told.
Within the pages of God's Holy Bible,
Is wisdom explaining this world's survival.

His will is not difficult to learn,
Love God and your fellow man in turn.
Love them by turning from your sin,
Embracing peace and love again.

Forgiveness lies within God's hands,
He sent His Son to cleanse our land;
With our eyes open we begin to see,
That the love of God is our only key.

Draw near to God and He will begin,
To free our land from its sin.
Living free we soon will see,
The peace of God from sea to sea.

1 Peter 4:8 *Above all, keep fervent in your love for one another, because love covers a multitude of sins.*

20 The Boiler

A boiling pot is not hot, under God's control.
While the pot boils, the cooks do toil,
Preparing feasts that feed the soul.

The cooks prepare the flesh to share,
On guests whom God bestows.
The water's fine, it's Christ's life from time,
Cleansing, washing, food for us here below.

The food prepared, in God's care,
Is palatable to all, I'm told.
God's word is true, He loves me and you,
Preparing meals that never grow old.

Prepared in time, for your life and mine,
We're invited to feasts reviving the soul.
It's Christ alive; the Bible our guide,
Prepared through ages long ago.

Christ was born and died, but then revived,
Rising to heights in heaven's control.
His word survives, a feast derived,
Giving life, a free gift, here below.

Living waters of life boil away our strife,
A feast for every soul,
Prepared by God for this earth we trod,
His word feeds us, making us grow.

John 6:27 *Jesus said, "Do not work for the food which perishes, but for the food which endures to eternal life....*

21 You are not alone

You are not alone, is the name of this poem,
You'll never walk in darkness again.
When you go to the light, it's our Lord's great delight,
To shine His word through the darkness of sin.

When dwelling in Christ, with His words your delight,
Light of His glory enters in.
Keep your heart in the Bible, so your mind is not libel,
And all you read is tendered within.

Psalms 119:11 *Your word I have treasured in my heart, that I may not sin against You.*

Rest

22 Peace at Rest

"Joy comes in the morning" is reconfirmed,
When we go to bed to comfort earned.
"How is this done," you might ask?
Through work of mind, heart and back.

A day's work is never done,
Until the setting of the sun.
Look around to observe,
Others working unperturbed.

A lot of work appears mundane,
Look again, it's not the same.
Work completed is peace regained,
Creating nights of calm sustained.

Joy in the morning is not a given,
It's through work accomplished among the living.
A job "well done" is not easily gained,
When bestowed by our Lord from His domain.

Psalms 30:5 *For His anger is but for a moment, His favor is for a lifetime; weeping may last for the night, but a shout of joy comes in the morning.*

23 Rest Decreed

Rest belongs to the Creator alone,
He can even create talking stones.
Walking our shores in times of old,
Our Creator's story is still retold.

His life on earth is readily seen,
Even by Hollywood's men who dream
His life extends within men's hearts,
Hidden in those needing restart.

That start begins in peace and rest,
Given by God to all His best.
Within this Land rest is in need,
By people, plants; all life decreed.

Rest is fleeting to those estranged,
From God's holy will unconstrained.
Rest is entrenched in hearts and minds,
Whose trust in God is by His design.

Psalms 37:3–7 *Trust in the LORD and do good; ... He will bring forth your righteousness as the light And your judgment as the noonday. Rest in the LORD and wait patiently for Him....*

24 God Rest

There is a time in the life of man,
When it seems the sun won't shine again.
In times of darkness you can see,
God's light beams forth eternally.

In His light we comprehend,
Life continues on again and again.
Each day renewed from dawn to dark,
Gives new strength to weakened hearts.

Strengthened, renewed from day to day,
We live in growing love to say;
"We love our spouse, family and friends,
Even our enemies when light enters in."

Love begins when we understand,
His love expands from man to man.
It begins in individual hearts,
Spreading to others creating sparks.

Each spark ignites a burning desire,
To light a fire in one another.
A warmth of kindness floods the soul,
When love expands in God's control.

We are tools in God's hand,
When in His love we begin again.
God rest is under His control,
When His love grows within our soul.

Hebrews 12:28–29 *Therefore, since we receive a kingdom which cannot be shaken, let us show gratitude, by which we may offer to God an acceptable service with reverence and awe; for our God is a consuming fire.*

25 A Day's Rest

Out of the lights into the night,
When a gentle rest is ordered.
It's again like night changing to light,
When by God's command sleep is over.

Life's windows open to a heavenly breeze,
Given rest we need by God's decree.
At the break of dawn we are strong,
With encouraging love we carry on.

Quietness of soul in God's control,
Is a quality to rely on.
We experience retreat in a good night's sleep,
Refreshed by God when our lives He keeps.

We are alive within God's eyes,
When His glory we see through His decrees,
When from our rest we do arise,
Awake in God's Son when we believe.

Hebrews 4:9–10 *So there remains a Sabbath rest for the people of God. For the one who has entered His rest has himself also rested from his works, as God did from His.*

26 Peace in Rest

There is a peace that transcends minds,
Available rest to all mankind.
Established by God from days of old,
A Sabbath rest for all, we're told.

Honor and respect to God who gives,
Life to all on this planet where we live.
Created by God, on the seventh day,
Then He rested that all of us might say:

Glory to God in the highest,
We sing His praises and pray.
Glory to God in the highest,
We worship Him every day.

Hebrews 4:9–10 *So there remains a Sabbath rest for the people of God. For the one who has entered His rest has himself also rested from his works, as God did from His.*

27 Dreams

Most dreams are not what they seem,
They are full of deception and error.
They are full of fluff to vanish as dust,
When reality blows away terror.

Dreams given in love from our God above,
Give peace and rest without measure.
Rest to each soul sent by God's control,
Will perfect peace of mind as a treasure.

Humorous dreams at night delight,
We could chuckle and laugh forever.
They make us smile for quite a while,
Their thoughts tickling like a feather.

Daytime dreams birth a man's schemes,
Of glory in honest endeavors.
But burst at the seams as reality screams,
"Wake up, dummy! You're getting better"

Ecclesiastes 5:7 *For in many dreams and in many words there is emptiness. Rather, fear God.*

28 Guiding Nights

Dreams at night can be a delight,
When guided by God's book of wisdom.
Draw near to God and talk out loud,
To your spouse before nightly oblivion.

You will see what's in store for thee,
Through friendly, loving discussions.
God's love for thee is dependent on she,
For she is key to God's love for thee.

I was drawn to she on bended knee,
Proposing my love to God and thee.
Faithfulness I vow to my frau,
When before God I kneel in awe.

It's God I see, when I please thee,
By duty, love and devotion.
It's you that I see in love with me,
In spite of my faults and emotions.

Song of Songs 6:10, 3 *Who is this that grows like the dawn,
As beautiful as the full moon, as pure as the sun, as awesome
as an army with banners? ...I am my beloved's and my beloved is mine*

29 Dreams and Things

Dreams and things that can't be seen,
The figments of the mind,
True reality above, the things we love,
That will not be left behind.

When with great care, we tarry there,
In the heavenlies with God's kind.
It's the earth we see through humanity,
That blesses and keeps us through time.

In time we see just who we will be,
In God's realm for those who believe.
It is God's great care to bless each hair,
On the heads of all conceived.

So worry not, the darkness has taught
All trained through their disbelief.
The light of day shows us the way,
To the Godhead and our relief.

Mark 9:23–24 *And Jesus said to him, "... All things are
possible to him who believes." Immediately the boy's father
cried out and said, "I do believe; help my
unbelief."*

30 Waters of Life

Living waters in flowing streams,
Swiftly go by as in a dream.
Rich waters of life available to you,
Free to drink for this earthly crew.

Christ came to earth to live and die,
Arising from the dead, being crucified.
The living water He foretold,
Emerged from His Spirit since days of old.

These waters of life you can readily see,
Rush out of hearts growing eternally.
Living waters, God's words of life,
Cascading upon us from paradise.

The place, we're planted to bloom and grow,
This place where waters forever flow.
Trees and plants grow beside each stream,
With beautifully living evergreens.

Full of life for all to behold,
Healing leaves of reds, greens and gold.
Drinking and drawing from each living stream,
Are the men and women who dare to dream.

John 7:37–38 *"He who believes in Me, as the Scripture said, 'From his innermost being will flow rivers of living water.'"*

31 Small Plots of Ground

Small plots of ground richly abound,
Over this planet we live on.
Some are for beauty, some grow grain,
Some inherently seem to know pain.

This land we see is you and me,
Beholden in the eye of destiny.
Even eyes of the blind can see just fine,
When by God's hand they are redesigned

For God clearly sees when we bend our knees,
And plead for things hard to believe.
In this rich ground our dreams are bound,
Discretely growing to soon be found.

To our surprise, dreams soon arise,
From seeds of things God's heart devised.
When Christ inspires they rise to the skies,
The fruits of beauty once denied.

It is God we see when on our knees,
With hope for future glory to be.
Our eyes see fine, which once were blind,
Restored to kindle the hearts of mankind.

John 9:5–7 *Jesus said to him, "Go, wash in the pool of Siloam" ... So he went away and washed, and came back seeing.*

32 Peace Will Reign

Peace will live in the hearts of men,
When love fully reigns once again.
Love at the home, business and play,
Will return again here to stay.

Love is not anxious, proud or pretentious,
Love is gentle, firm and condescendious.
Love can be rough but kind and tough,
In the hands of those who know their stuff.

Love is meaningful in those who obey,
God command's, "Love your neighbor today"
Love is kind to those of His mind,
Formed by our Savior's direction and time.

Take time to learn to love and obey,
All that our Christ told us during His stay.
The Bible, His word, we can trust and say,
"Peace for my soul and family, today."

Malachi 2:6 *...he walked with Me in peace and uprightness, and he turned many back from iniquity.*

CREATION

Land

33 Lightning Bugs

Lightning shooting across the sky,
Dancing, shimmering as it flies by.
Wiggling deep into the grass,
Erupting abruptly in sight at last.

Lightning of life flashing on and off,
Boldly exposing them to the lost.
Each man and woman in Christ doth shine,
Like lightning bugs in hearts and minds.

Rising above gray doom and gloom,
Lighting each life when given room.
Full light of life is granted by God,
When in His Son's footsteps we daily trod.

Dancing and shimmering wherever they go,
Christians, like lightning bugs, shine here below.
Glowing and glimmering in darkness they're found,
God's representatives on earth here abound.

John 8:12 *Then Jesus again spoke to them, saying, "I am the Light of the world; he who follows Me will not walk in the darkness, but will have the Light of life."*

34 Newness of Life

Spring is green,
Winter is white,
Fall is golden,
Summer a delight.

God is love,
Heaven is bright,
The Son is beholden,
His earth made right.

Enjoy God's creation,
Earth and sea,
His mercy and grace,
Loved by you and me.

Behold God's gift,
A Son is given,
Believe in Him,
Our pathway to heaven.

2 Corinthians 5:17 *Therefore if anyone is in Christ, he is a new creature; the old things passed away; behold, new things have come.*

35 Epicenter

The center of our continent,
Gives delightful confidence;
That our Creator lives in this land.

Look unto rich growing grain,
Where land and sky seem just the same;
Blended and meeting in one band,
Flowing uniformly across our land.

The sky descends touching the grain,
With golden heavenly light sustained;
And grain ascends from earth to sky,
Melding colors together from on high.

It is easy to see that God loves thee,
When looking creatively at all we see;
Godly proof flows from heaven above,
Sustained on our earthly planet in love.

The town of Rugby is small and serene,
Built by God's people, bright and clean;
Centered on earth; a heavenly band.

Psalms 11:7 *For the LORD is righteous, He loves righteousness; The upright will behold His face.*

36 Birds, Trees and We

A calliope of branches and golden leaves,
Bending and blowing in the breeze.
Aspen, maple and stately oak,
Tuned to the sounds of bubbling brooks.

Warblers, robins and turtle doves,
Singing to our God reigning above.
Nestled amongst hardwoods and pines,
Sounds forth music pure and sublime.

On a good day for all to see,
Birds of paradise singing to Thee.
Songs of worship and glorious praise,
To the Creator by whom they were made.

Given to mankind to have and to hold,
Birds and trees sing loudly and bold.
All songs go forth in blessed release,
A calliope in tune by nature's decree.

Psalms 104:10, 12 *He sends forth springs in the valleys…*
Beside them the birds of the heavens dwell; They lift up their
voices among the branches.

37 God's Glory Shines

From the beginning of time God's word resounds,
From hills, valleys and streams all vibrantly found.
From mountains grand and canyons deep,
Your world is proof of Your word and deeds.

We exalt you O' Lord above highest hills,
Your word in the sound of rivers and trills.
Declaring Your glory, wisdom and might,
Through sun still shining clear and bright.

Page upon page carved on hearts untold
Your glory's revealed in lives exposed,
Exposed for nations to exultantly see,
Your glory and mercy spread from sea to sea.

The lives of men, though hidden, serene,
Are being transformed into what is now seen.
Lives lived in darkness are now being revealed,
Showing their harshness, refined or disheveled.

Other lives show that gentleness reigns,
When light of the life of God's Son is maintained.
Sorrow and troubles flee from within,
When the work of God's Son is allowed to begin.

The heavens declare God's glory again,
When lives are freed from the burdens of sin.
The oceans and streams are blessed by His love,
When our hearts, as stewards, are cleansed from above.

Isaiah 2:2–3 ... *And many peoples will come and say,*
"Come, let us go up to the mountain of the LORD, to the
house of the God of Jacob....

38 Filtered Light

It's raining now, the sky's gray somehow,
But plants are growing, the cattle lowing.

The trees are bending, the winds are ending,
The leaves all turning, the rivers churning.

Marshes and trees are a delight to see,
The forest light ends the night.

Spring will come with the sun,
The heavens now open in His devotion.

It's God we see through earth and trees,
Here to stay is the light of His day.

Proverbs 16:15 *In the light of a king's face is life, and his favor is like a cloud with the spring rain.*

39 Harmony

Living in harmony with all we see,
Is God's plan for you and me.

Forests and marsh, crop, pasture and brush,
All sustain life for people like us.

Birds of the sky, creatures of land and seas,
All are sustained by the God we cannot see.

But our Creator exists in all we behold,
Under the heavens of blues, reds and golds.

May all who see be led by God's light,
Known as sons and daughters of His delight.

This land we love, cherish and care for,
Is worth living our earthly life for.

Nehemiah 9:20–21 *You gave Your good Spirit to instruct them...You gave them water for their thirst. Indeed, forty years You provided for them in the wilderness and they were not in want....*

40 Cleansed

Though doubts and worries may plague the day,
Prayer at night chases each away.
When we worry we expose our sin,
Though it may not reflect our heart within.

Our soul within can be freed from sin,
Since Christ died for our man within.
The storms of life are not in control,
Cures arise from His life in our soul.

When doubts arrive, look to the skies,
The sun still shines, the stars still rise.
Look to the deep within your soul,
You will find out God's still in control.

Water God's seeds that make you whole,
Flowers will bloom nearly out of control.
Sweet scents wafting in this world we know,
Cleansed by Christ washing whiter than snow.

Acts 11:9 *But a voice from heaven answered a second time, 'What God has cleansed, no longer consider unholy.'*

Water

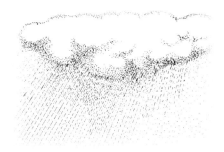

41 Snow Flowers

When traveling roads in nature we see,
The love of God from eternity.
Flats, valleys and hills all covered in snow,
Herald spring's coming again, I truly know.

Flowers are silently, anticipating growth,
Buried in white depths two feet below.
Twisting and turning, seeking the sun,
Small shoots of life are just now begun.

Life isn't restricted to things now exposed,
But is stretching, growing,
Under a cover of snow.
The Son again encourages new life,
To sprout high above this world's inherited strife.

Look to the Son for the glory to see,
Under blankets of snow tenderly conceived.
Life once again gently blossoms and grows,
When finally released from winter's snow.

Song of Songs 2:11–12 *For behold, the winter is past, the
rain is over and gone. The flowers have already appeared in
the land....*

42 Snow

Softly falls the snow all gentle and white,
Covering earth's browns with purest delight.
Plumes sparkling white spread in God's love,
Drift down from dark branches up high above.

White and dark contrasts side by side,
Reveal God's goodness where we reside.
Yet heaven and earth will pass away,
Like snowflakes on earth not here to stay.

Enjoy God's cleansing white as this snow,
With Him someday eternally we'll go.
The snow will pass, its beauty remain,
In hearts pure white by His Son maintained.

When you see snow falling clean and white,
Look up to God and in Him delight.
He'll always cleanse us whiter than snow,
When in His Son's image we're committed to go.

Psalms 51:7 *Purify me with hyssop, and I shall be clean;
Wash me, and I shall be whiter than snow.*

43 Shimmering and Glimmering

Shimmering and glimmering all through the night,
Snowflakes sparkle in morning's first light.
Dawn now breaks in purest white,
New snow has fallen to our delight.

New white on muddy, faded dirt and leaves,
Brings freshness to our world of needs.
Gone are worries, troubles and woes,
As they disappear behind new fallen snow.

White covers browns and blacks in trees,
Refreshes our lives like a cool winter breeze.
Gone are aging chins, cheeks and hair,
Replaced by rosebuds to lives so fair.

Holy, holy, all things dressed in white,
Cleansed by our Creator to His delight.
Gone is all dirt from past trouble and sin,
Turned white forever by His work within.

Isaiah 1:18 *"Come now, and let us reason together," says the
Lord, "Though your sins are as scarlet, they
will be as white as snow…"*

44 Raindrops and Rainbows

Raindrops and rainbows go hand in hand,
And our God still rules in this great land.
Though rain brings hurt and pain to some,
The life it brings blesses everyone.

Life without water would be hell on earth,
Life without rainbows depressing or worse.
Drought might occur as an unwanted host,
God brings rain abundantly to most.

Floods drown many a person's dreams,
Water rushing down numerous streams.
To some a disaster, to others new growth,
Green plants reaching clear to heaven's hosts.

Floods and showers go hand in hand,
Life renewed all over this land.
Correction and rewards, result when we try,
For both storms and plenty raise hands on high,

Job 37:11–13 *Also with moisture He loads the thick cloud; He disperses the cloud of His lightning. It changes direction, turning around by His guidance, that it may do whatever He commands it on the face of the inhabited earth. Whether for correction, or for His world, or for loving kindness, He causes it to happen.*

45 Still Fishing

Sunshine and pleasure are here to behold,
Winter is past, spring and summer unfold.
Warmth of the sun lifts up our souls,
Spirits soar high with absence of cold

Anticipation of water to wiggle your toes,
Fish nibbling at hairs on bare legs below.
Visions of dining on warm water delights,
That pleasantly drift out of your sight.

Dining on air becomes normal for most;
While fishing the deep for our watery host.
Try as we may fish often escape,
The heat of the pan and a clean dinner plate.

The wiliest of Evangels on earth today,
Are fishing for men for the kingdom's sake.
Led by God they cast out His word,
Build upon hope their salvation secured.

Mark 1:17 *And Jesus said to them, "Follow Me, and I will make you become fishers of men."*

46 Smile

Rain in one's life is not a disaster,
Tempered by God it grows the hereafter.
Rain you will see is no travesty,
It begins new life eternally.

The eternal God causes flowers to grow,
While rain just simply renews each soul.
Heavenly drops pour down earthly strife,
Which free us to handle tests in our life.

Whatever you see is by God's decree,
Flowers and trees for you and me.
Pain and strife are part of life,
Hidden in minds, meant for sheer delight.

What you see growing in me,
Is God's love planned from eternity.
Rain and sun have taken their toll,
Smiles shine forth from within the soul.

Psalms 147:7–8 *Sing to the Lord with thanksgiving... Who covers the heavens with clouds, Who provides rain for the earth, Who makes grass to grow on the mountains.*

47 Rainbows

Rainbows in spring are clear and clean,
Rainbows in fall are infrequent, if at all.
Rainbows in winter? When temps are bitter.
Rainbows in summer abound without number.

Rain and rainbows go hand and hand,
Clouds and storms thunder over land.
Left in their wake are flowers and springs,
Bubbling forth colors; refreshing things.

Rainbows in heavens and on earth below,
Colors splashed high, the skies are aglow,
Colorful flowers amidst grasses green.
Vibrant promises of God foreseen.

Rainbows delight all those who have sight,
No more floods to fear, its God we revere.
God's promise is seen on the firmament above,
A covenant was given to all by God's love.

Genesis 9:14–15 *It shall come about, when I bring a cloud over the earth, that the bow will be seen in the cloud, ... and never again shall the water become a flood to destroy all flesh.*

48 Showers and Rainbows

Showers arrive amongst beams of light,
And Rainbows bring on sheer delight.
Night showers arise making things grow,
Sun in the morning brightens each soul.

Daytime storms may dampen the heart,
But when they are gone, life restarts.
Living water implants new life,
Flowing from the Son of Light.

The Bread of Life sits on His throne,
Caring for all who are His own.
We're never abandoned or forsaken,
Even when our world is shaken.

Though quakes and floods seem to never end,
Suddenly, we're born again.
Rain and rainbows blessed by the Son,
Restore new hope for everyone.

Romans 5:2–5...*we exult in hope of the glory of God. And not only this, but we also exult in our tribulations, knowing that tribulation brings about perseverance; and perseverance, proven character; and proven character, hope; and hope does not disappoint....*

49 Sunshine and Rain

Sunshine and rain are one and the same,
Restoring joy to lives reclaimed
Sunshine for beauty, our features enhanced,
Rain for longevity, as God commands.

Strength and beauty emerge from the soul,
When grown by God under His control.
Gently a life does glow and shine,
Refreshed by God in our hearts through time.

Rain is good for each one's soul,
When given by God under His control.
Length of days can be maintained,
When we seek God in our hurt and pain.

The light of life shines from within,
Though watered by strife in this world of sin.
The heavens extend our life that remains,
God's gifts emerge from sunshine and rain.

Isaiah 9:2 *The people who walk in darkness will see a great light; those who live in a dark land, the light will shine on them.*

50 Spring Shower

Hearts that are heavy tired and worn,
Need God's love as shelters from storms.
True rain falls on hearts softened by God,
The waters of life descend from above.

God's rain nurtures our new, growing lives,
Freeing them from scars of sin and strife.
Rain begins growing new seeds from within,
From God's word sown by holy men.

Life once more yearns to begin,
Within life's seeds now free from sin.
Seeds that grow with each passing shower,
Strengthened by God's might and power.

Lightning and thunder abound in one's life,
When new growth is nurtured to God's delight.
Pleasant calm returns from time to time,
When in God's love the sun again shines.

Yes, sun shines once again in hearts,
When from their sin men do depart.
Cast out bad seed once freely sown,
From the tempter's store of weeds and thorns.

But plants that are nurtured by His loving care,
Grow good seed cast when our lives we share.
Each life grown to maturity and strength,
Repeats the process that God began.

1 Peter 1:22–23 *for you have been born again not of seed which is perishable but imperishable, that is, through the living and enduring word of God.*

Sky

51 Breaking of Day

Pinks and whites, blues and grays,
Heralds in the break of day,
Pink clouds drift in soft blue skies,
Reveal God's wisdom before our eyes.

The dawn of life we now can see,
Created by God from eternity.
Out of the darkness, from within His depths,
Exploding from wombs of righteousness.

New life begins in hearts restored,
Whenever God's hand is holding yours,
You'll grow and see what's in store for thee,
For God chose you from eternity.

He invites us to choose life over death,
Guided by God we're put to the test.
Refined through the fires of calamity,
We'll shine like the sun eternally.

In God's Sonshine we will finally see.
Life dawning above mountains, and over the seas.
Reds, pinks and blues amidst golden light,
Raise bright hopes beyond human sight.

Daniel 12:3 *Those who have insight will shine brightly like
the brightness of the expanse of heaven, and those
who lead the many to righteousness, like the
stars forever and ever.*

52 Sparkle

The darkness of night can be delight,
When viewed through the glory of God.
Look to the stars, they glisten and glimmer,
Placed by God's hand to guide lost sinners.

Where do we start? Try forsaking the sin,
That you nurtured, coddled but despised.
How do we know when our sin will go?
By turning to God we get His surprise.

Gone they will be buried deep in the sea,
Removed forever far from you and me.
God expresses His mercy in all that He sees,
Forgiving my sins once held dear to me.

God is the One who loves you and me,
As we earnestly seek on bended knees.
Then when your mind is quiet and heart is light,
He'll be as bright as heaven sparkling at night.

Psalms 19:1 *The heavens are telling of the glory of God;
and their expanse is declaring the work of His hands.*

53 Star Shine

On cold winter nights stars shine extra bright,
Appearing to shiver and dance in the cold.
Brightness is enhanced in the young by romance,
Cuddled together in youthful vigor bold.

They look to the skies with wide open eyes,
Sensing what the heavens seem to hold.
It's the promise of things seldom seen,
Peering through windows of the soul.

What do they see in the sky dark blue,
That I have seen many times before?
Everything seems new to hearts that are true,
Lived in sight of heavens open door.

The heavens declare God's glory each day,
Bask in His love as we serve and obey.
To each one is given His heavenly wisdom,
Shining brightly like stars when we pray.

Psalms 8:3–4 *When I consider Your heavens, the work of
Your fingers, the moon and the stars, which You have
ordained; what is man that You take thought of him, and the
son of man that You care for him?*

54 The Night Sky

What appears to some is hidden from others,
The light of life for sisters and brothers.
Alive in Christ is paradise to some,
A challenge, at best, to others becomes.

When in halls of darkness we reside,
Our thoughts in Christ are still glorified.
We lift our eyes unto the stars,
From where our God is never far.

The stars are more than bright specks of light,
They are God's Gospel from paradise.
The stars are not silent as some would think,
They speak the deep message of writer's ink.

Those who write to the glory of God,
Touch their pens in our Savior's blood.
His glory is found throughout the earth,
Excelling in heavenly skies He birthed.

James 1:17 *Every good thing given and every perfect gift is from above, coming down from the Father of lights, with whom there is no variation or shifting shadow.*

55 Rainbow Seeking

Dear God of peace that transcends minds,
Come live within this heart of mine.
Not all in here is bright and cheery,
Some days are dreadful, dark and dreary.

But on days like this we lift You on high,
We raise our heads unto the skies.
Gladness reigns when it's You we seek,
And sadness flees with Your release.

Rainbows bend across the heavens,
When from Your storehouse rain is given.
Rain makes life abundantly grow,
In hearts alive on this plane below.

The heavens declare Your glory, Lord,
When Your hands release rich treasure stores.
Skies glow golden, warming men's hearts.
When through His Son, hope He imparts.

Psalms 19:1 *The heavens are telling of the glory of God; and their expanse is declaring the work of His hands.*

56 The Firmament

The sky is clear and tranquil,
The stars sparkle again.
The moon beckons to lovers,
To those forsaking their sin.

The air we breathe was purchased,
At, oh, so great a price.
Cleansed by our God still living,
Through His Son sacrificed.

He paid the price at Calvary,
Where He died upon the tree.
He rose again from the dead,
To give us life great and free.

We now can live, roam and breathe,
With our heads again held high.
We reach into the heavenlies,
Holy hands touching the sky.

Alive we breathe in God's love,
Enjoying all He created.
We are drawn to Him through His Son,
To share His world much underrated.

We are free in Christ to live and breathe,
Bringing praise to our Savior.
By all our actions, words and deeds,
We worship our Creator.

Psalms 19:1 (KJV) *The heavens declare the glory of God;*
and the firmament showeth his handiwork.

57 Flight of Grace

The birds above shine through the skies,
Beyond what human eyes describe.
God endows them with wings of grace,
Permitting flight from place to place.

We can likewise soar at times,
When in God's grace we do shine.
Christ arose to live in us,
Giving us wings instead of dust.

When we arise within His light,
We also soar above our fright.
Rising o'er each and every storm,
Our God reigns when we're reborn.

The soul residing in my heart,
Often needs a brand new start.
When His flame warms our wings,
Life is not what it often seems.

Beginning flight always begins,
By daily casting off our sin.
When in doubt we bring our eyes,
To God's true word that never dies.

God's word allowed to enter in,
Restores our lives now free of sin.
Then our strong wings unfold in flight,
Rising above the fears of night.

Isaiah 40:31 *Yet those who wait for the Lord will gain new strength; they will mount up with wings like eagles....*

58 Sonshine, Earthshine and the Stars

The creation days have ended,
God's Son has since descended
He suffered and died that we might arise,
With Him to the glories of paradise.

His kingdom is eternal,
The heavens are His journal.
Look to the skies, you cannot deny,
The stars declare His enterprise.

The firmament declares His beauty,
Sustained through His life and duty.
The clouds above His earth sustained,
By the wisdom of His holy name.

The majesty of cedar and pine,
He planted on this earth so kind.
Growing for humanity to use and see,
When we act in faith intelligently.

This earth we walk upon,
Gives life to all His sons.
We grow most by what we eat,
When fed true words at Jesus' feet.

God lives within the oceans deep,
Created for all life on earth to keep.
The waves above, and their quiet below,
His storms of life calm us deep in our soul.

God's Son is living here to stay,
He will not forsake you any day.
God's work is true and lives through you,
When you love and trust and obey.

Genesis 1:1–3 *In the beginning God created the heavens and the earth. The earth was formless and void, and darkness was over the surface of the deep, and the Spirit of God was moving over the surface of the waters. Then God said, "Let there be...."*

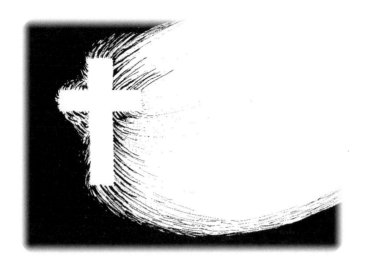

LIGHT

59 The Light I Know

Even the pit's depth, is a place of rest,
When under God's control.
All that we know of life here below,
Is a given by God who bestows.

In the pit's depth, He teaches us best,
To trust in the God of our soul.
From the depths we are blessed,
Completing God's test,
Bearing light to this world here below.

The light is not mine, but borrowed through time,
From Christ who restores life's souls.
The light given by God on this earth He trod,
Shines in each person He knows.

When we follow each spark alive in the dark,
That we find in the night of our soul,
Each spark becomes flame, when in Christ's name,
We tell others what we know.

John 8:12 *Then Jesus again spoke to them, saying,*
"I am the Light of the world; he who follows Me will not
walk in the darkness, but will have the Light of life."

60 God's Light Dawning

The morning light does now excite,
Our hearts abound with gladness.
Beside my wife I do delight,
In dawn arising from dark nights.

As dawn breaks forth, I can perceive,
That truth in life lies in God's light.
His light dispels all fears conceived,
Once those born blind their sight received.

Blinded from birth by original sin,
Mankind learns God's plans unfolding.
Hearts seared and scarred so harsh and deep,
Now show God's love being released.

His Son gave away a tortured life,
That the world could begin to see,
A new world arising from the night,
Within God's glorious revealing sight.

The effects of sin within God's world,
Are forever revealed and broken,
By obedience to God's inerrant word,
Which through His Son was spoken.

John 8:12 *Then Jesus again spoke to them, saying, "I am the Light of the world; he who follows Me will not walk in the darkness, but will have the Light of life."*

61 Into God's Light

Out of the darkness of the night,
Into a future bathed in light.
Sunshine and flowers side by side,
Chasing out darkness like the tide.

The firmament frames the children of light,
Firmly standing to God's delight.
The heavenly realm declares the story,
God's children living with Christ in glory.

Days of darkness will be forgiven,
Heaven reveals the glories for living.
Earth and sea blended in strength,
Framed by rainbows abounding in length.

Life begins beyond earth's skin,
When in repentance we turn to Him.
Then life and light in us remains,
As by His love we are maintained.

Ezekiel 1:28 *As the appearance of the rainbow in the clouds on a rainy day, so was the appearance of the surrounding radiance. Such was the appearance of the likeness of the glory of the Lord....*

62 Silently

Silently, silently, silent as night,
Out of our darkness into God's light.
Into the brightness of each shining star,
Shining from heaven so near yet so far.

Love shines from heaven to us here on earth,
Bathed in sunlight are those of rebirth.
Beyond the fog, the rain and the snow,
We look, and behold, His promised rainbow.

Life without hope exists not on earth,
For salt and light live within the rebirth.
God does not leave us depressed and alone,
Within His love our hope is reborn.

So call upon God while He is near,
The day may come when He will not hear.
Yet he always hears those born from above,
Changed by His infinite, unending love.

Isaiah 55:6 *Seek the Lord while He may be
found; call upon Him while He is near.*

63 The Light of Day

The light of day was never so bright,
As the light of Christ that cuts through night.
Our hearts and minds get dull with worry,
For family and friends in a big hurry.

Designed by God, the Christian heart,
Is welded to Christ's to never depart.
When in the darkness we lift voices and shout,
"Our God reigns!" There is no doubt.

We call upon Him for all our needs,
Fear dissolves in a summer breeze.
Once destined for death again we arrive,
At the cross of Christ we once denied.

Christ reigns in lives lived for Him,
Our family and friends may enter in.
Our fear is gone once more replaced,
By life in Christ and His saving grace.

Revelation 19:6 ...*Hallelujah! For the Lord our God, the Almighty, reigns.*

64 Light in the Night

Two friends I see, in need I perceive,
They have and are holding together.
The bind that ties is the light in their eyes,
From the life of Him living forever.

Christ alone is our cornerstone,
They build their house on the Rock together.
Together they stand, a three-stranded band,
Enduring storms with Christ as their tether.

Limited by God, is this earth that they trod,
Surviving trials seeming to go on forever.
One burden begins where the other one ends,
Tunnel light does not seem to get better.

It is in the park and out of the dark,
God's glorious light shines on them together.
A walk in the park of God's loving heart,
Reveals sights and smells like flowering heather.

The aroma to some may benumb,
Being the fragrance of salvation to others.
God's children arise under this world's skies,
Beholding God's Son Jesus Christ, together.

John 8:12 *Then Jesus again spoke to them, saying, "I am the Light of the world; he who follows Me will not walk in the darkness, but will have the Light of life."*

65 Rehab

Society needs its people,
All members short and tall.
We're in this life together,
Our God created us all.

When this world's strife darkens lives,
We turn to those in whom God delights.
They turn our frowns into smiling clowns,
Laughter replaces looking down.

Joy abounds in the God of love,
Granted to each seeking that above.
When our hearts refill with love again,
Pain retreats to where it began.

Lost in darkness not to return,
The light of life brightly burns.
A shining glow for all to see,
As we head toward God's eternity.

Created in love by our God we know,
His eternal flame warms hearts below.
Rising within His heavenly light,
Our spirits soar with great delight.

Matthew 12:20–21 (KJV) *A bruised reed shall he not break, and smoking flax shall he not quench, till he send forth judgment unto victory. And in his name shall the Gentiles trust.*

66 New Birth

Long ago in time, the sun did not shine,
Created light came by God's design.
Growing with the rising of the sun,
Created new life has now begun.

The light of the Son in hearts does arise,
Like the morning star to our surprise.
Again, new life is daily begun,
In the heart of every chosen one.

Born again we are renewed,
To join a celestial working crew.
Each one lives to God on high,
Because God's Son was crucified.

Destined to live eternally,
The concept of life is sacred to me.
Lives now defined by God's design,
Throughout this world so brightly shine.

John 3:5–6 *Jesus answered, "Truly, truly, I say to you, unless one is born of water and the Spirit he cannot enter into the kingdom of God. That which is born of the flesh is flesh, and that which is born of the Spirit is spirit."*

67 God Rest

There is a time in the life of man,
When it seems the sun may not shine again.
But even in darkness you can see,
God's light beams forth eternally.

In His light we comprehend,
Life continues again and again.
Each day renewed from dawn to dark,
Gives new strength to weakened hearts.

Strengthened, renewed from day to day,
We carry on in love to say;
"We love our spouse, family and friends,
Even our enemies as light enters in."

Love begins when we understand,
His love expands from man to man.
Beginign in individual hearts,
Creating sparks when it departs.

Each spark ignites a burning desire,
To light a fire in one another.
A warmth of kindness floods the soul,
When love expands in God's control.

We are tools in God's own hand,
When in His love we begin again.
God's rest is under His control,
When His love grows within our soul.

Job 33:29–30 *Behold, God does all these oftentimes with men, to bring back his soul from the pit, that he may be enlightened with the light of life.*

68 Night Light

When nights seem difficult and days are tough,
We rise in the morning thinking, I've had enough.
I return to bed to shut out the light,
And revel in comforts of resuming night.

Daylight, once dawned, glows in the dark,
Fades to oblivion as the world becomes stark.
Life's difficulties seen in early morning light,
Are no challenge to those in whom God delights.

The dawning of light in this world reveals,
Opportunities for growing tall, unconcealed.
Standing tall in God's created world of light,
Opens new horizons within our sight.

Visions of light our good God unfolds,
Upon friends and foes His grace He bestows.
With eyes wide open and out of the night,
The deeds of darkness no longer delight.

God is impartial to whom He restarts,
The light of His grace in each man's heart.
The home of the dead is unveiled by God's light,
It no longer belongs to the dreads of the night.

God's light of life shines through lives born again,
Making darkness and light both inherently our friend.
The light of day reveals challenges of delight,
Bringing joys in our work within God's sight.

Colossians 3:23 *Whatever you do, do your work heartily, as for the Lord....*

69 A Days Rest

Out of the lights into the night,
When a gentle rest is ordered,
It is again like night changing to light,
When by God's command sleep is over.

Life's windows open to a heavenly breeze,
Giving needed rest by God's decree.
At the break of dawn we are strong,
With encouraging love we carry on.

Quietness of soul in God's control,
Is a quality we rely on.
We'll experience a retreat in a good night's sleep,
Refreshed by God when our lives He doth keep.

We soon arise within God's eyes,
His glory we see through His decrees,
When from our rest He does release,
Awake in God's Son; His will be done!

Hebrews 4:9–10 *So there remains a Sabbath rest for the people of God. For the one who has entered His rest has himself also rested from his works, as God did from His.*

70 Light and Life

God's work is not through until He's dealt with you,
For all the errors of your ways.
Can't you now see how He cares for thee,
Tenderly, when you obey?

Never depart, draw near to God's heart,
When life's burdens tend to waylay.
God's light is pure, clean and bright,
Restoring hope to the darkest of nights.

You'll never fear when God's love draws near,
For each request as we pray.
Our fears and doubts vanish with shouts,
For victory over sin and decay.

Our walk through life is a delight,
When walking by His light each day.
It is Christ who shines in hearts and minds,
As His Nature shows us the way.

John 8:12 *Then Jesus again spoke to them, saying, "I am the Light of the world; he who follows Me will not walk in the darkness, but will have the Light of life."*

71 Light in the Darkness

The children of light walk into the night,
Reveling in auroras of hope before them
Darkness can't claim those in His holy name,
Christ's light destroys shadows before Him.

The darkness of night is no longer a fright,
To the children on earth who surround us.
Each child of God on this earth daily trods,
By the daylight shining around us.

By the light of Christ we see into the night,
Through God's book open before us.
The Bible beams bright bringing darkness to light,
When God's words of life restores us.

When drawn out of night, by His holy light,
We embrace God's truths shining before us.
He won't let us go through trials, troubles or woes,
Until we've arrived at home to adore Him.

Psalms 97:11 *Light is sown like seed for the righteous and gladness for the upright in heart.*

72 Light Out of Darkness

There is a day in the life of man,
When it seems the sun won't shine again.
Trials, troubles, health and death,
Form in your soul as a test.

Never, never stop your striving,
Arise, clean up, continue trying.
The darkness lightens an inch at a time,
When in God's word we read line upon line.

Despondency ends when in our ears,
We hear God shout, "Do not fear!"
From His Bible these words do form,
Our hearts are nurtured when we're reborn.

Joy comes with morning light,
When in His world we find delight.
Look unto earth, its flowers and trees,
Our God reigns in all you see.

Victory is gained over death and sin,
When in our life Christ is let in.
He now remains in our life to stay,
Bringing the light of life to each day.

1 Kings 8:59–60 *And may these words of mine, with which I have made supplication before the Lord, be near to the Lord our God day and night....*

73 Seekers and Finders

Seekers and finders, God's kingdom before,
Past sins hidden behind tightly closed doors.
Darkness is now an element past,
God's light in our lives arrives here at last.

Darkness must flee in spite of old sins,
The light of Christ's life now begins.
Forgiveness must not be taken for granted,
Christ died on the cross for all disadvantaged.

Born again gives no grounds to boast,
New life is something Christ gracefully bestows.
Life given to all, repentant of sins,
Revealing not new life outward, but totally within.

God's light reveals to the world's castaways,
Better things to see for the rest of our days.
New life begins in each person's heart,
When by God's Spirit His love imparts.

Hebrews 11:6 *And without faith it is impossible to please Him, for he who comes to God must believe that He is and that He is a rewarder of those who seek Him.*

74 A New Song

The sun is rising, the moon declining,
And our hearts are burning within.
The night has refreshed our tired flesh,
A new blessed day now begins.

The light shines true in each life renewed,
By the Creator of this world we live in.
We rise to work, and do not shirk,
What God in His wisdom has given.

The world of the living, results in each giving,
Glory to God as we're daily restored.
Each one does arise, to the world's surprise,
As hope flows to those He adores.

When we joyfully give, to all who live,
A "Good morning!" or cheery "Hello!"
We present by our life, songs of paradise,
To all living on earth here below.

Matthew 13:52 *And Jesus said to them, "Therefore every scribe who has become a disciple of the kingdom of heaven is like a head of a household, who brings out of his treasure things new and old."*

75 Discernment

Judgment day is here to stay;
No figment of our imagination.
The trials we see are meant to be;
Pathways building good discernment.

Every day we live our God gives;
Us life to brighten our way.
By His light we see eternally,
When we do not stray away.

Philippians 1:9–10 *And this I pray, that your love may abound still more and more in real knowledge and all discernment, so that you may approve the things that are excellent, in order to be sincere and blameless until the day of Christ;*

CHIMES

MUSIC

76 Music in the Air

There is music in the air,
Melodic strains beyond compare.
'Nearer my God to thee,' rings round about,
Heavenly voices sing and the earth shouts.

The music of God is clearly discerned,
Rolling water, bubbling brooks amidst ferns.
Wind whistling and dancing among stately pine,
Joyfully blessing God-filled minds.

God's peace is heard through fields and glades,
With flowers and green grass rolling in waves.
His voice resounds in thundering crash,
Amidst wind and rain in each lightning flash.

God's love for man is brought through His Son,
Who lived and died for everyone.
No greater music was ever proclaimed,
Than when we call out, "In Jesus name!"

Heavens wisdom comes in unfailing notes,
Rising in waves from praising throats.
Music that springs from heaven to earth,
Living within those newly rebirthed.

Mark 4:39 *And Jesus got up and rebuked the wind and said to the sea, "Hush, be still." And the wind died down and it became perfectly calm.*

77 Sing a Joyous Song

When you sing a joyous song unto the Lord,
Your faith and hope will be restored.
All dread of darkness flees away,
As God's light and glory saves each day.

God's Son is light in hearts and minds,
Renewed within each life divine.
His glory shines from lives once in darkness
Now revealing light in contrasting sharpness.

Let your light shine in song and dance,
Boldly go forth, your life is enhanced.
Shining from above through your life,
When Filtered by God your a living delight.

Light of the world reigns on high,
Heaven and earth will not deny.
God's face in you shines from above,
Reflected joyfully through His love.

Matthew 5:16 *Jesus said, "Let your light shine before men in such a way that they may see your good works, and glorify your Father who is in heaven.*

78 Something Old, Something New

Life goes on in a new song,
Orchestrated by Christ the King.
Our King of Glory does respond,
In human hearts His music rings.

"The King of Glory does come in!
The King of Glory does come in!
Who is this King of Glory?
Who is this King of Glory?"

"The Lord of Hosts,
He is the King of Glory,"
The Christ is His name!
His glory is the old, old story.

He has risen into glory,
Recorded in lives over time.
Human hearts revealing His story,
Transformed by His design.

Titus 3:5 *He saved us, not on the basis of deeds which we have done in righteousness, but according to His mercy, by the washing of regeneration and renewing by the Holy Spirit*

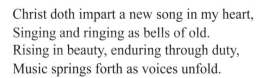

79 A Song in My Heart

Christ doth impart a new song in my heart,
Singing and ringing as bells of old.
Rising in beauty, enduring through duty,
Music springs forth as voices unfold.

Heartfelt songs shared by a throng,
Reverberating from hearts, minds and souls.
Kindred spirits singing forth lyrics,
Ordained by God's control.

Now living on earth, alive by rebirth,
Our God reigns, orchestrating each soul.
Sweet voices rise, to their surprise,
Resounding beauty, echoed here below.

Joyfully singing, heaven's bells ringing,
Musical sounds out of each soul.
Guided in love by our Savior above,
Stars shining and bowing low.

Job 38:7 *When the morning stars sang together and all the sons of God shouted for joy?*

80 A Song in the Dawn

With a song on our lips,
We wake to life's bliss.
As shrouds of dark nights,
Flee at new light.

Daylight grows bright,
With heavenly light,
When in God's word,
Living music is heard.

Going forth in the dawn,
With hearts full of song,
Brings light to our life,
As we walk in delight.

God's word lightens our path,
With songs that do last.
Music enters God's light,
Birthed in our dark nights.

Shades of darkness are past,
As we reach home at last.
God's light shows the way,
Walking into His day.

John 12:35 *So Jesus said to them, "For a little while longer the Light is among you. Walk while you have the Light...."*

81 Sing Along

There is a time in the life of man,
When God alone makes him stand.
We bow our knees when we do hear,
His heart's cry sounding on our deafened ear.

Our hearts are now turned to Christ our king,
His words that make all nations sing.
When in our hearts He alone does reign,
Unity is restored in our lives again.

Within our families, life is renewed,
Spreading outward to all who choose.
A life-style taught us by our King,
Once again all hearts will sing.

Songs of worship and of praise,
Rising to our King all days.
Music arising from within,
Each soul released from former sin.

Psalms 146:2 *I will praise the LORD while I live; I will sing praises to my God while I have my being.*

82 Melody, Rap and Memories

Songs arise in the hearts of those who believe,
It doesn't come from you or me.

The song arises from the depths of soul,
From hidden recesses that God only knows.

The song may be melodic with words of peace,
Bouncing from heart to heart to never cease.

They may be songs of strength, grace and hope,
Soaring to heights known by each soul.

Songs of purpose lift those who forgive,
Yet from the depths arise new hope to live.

Pop, blues, rap, classic sounds, I'm told,
When done in love refresh both young and old.

Glad sounds of music brought to your ear,
Are what our God wants you to hear.

These sounds anchor us to where we are,
While dwelling beneath God's brightest stars.

Job 38:7 *When the morning stars sang together and all the sons of God shouted for joy?*

83 A New Start

A song in your heart is a good start,
To begin each and every day.
If what you love comes from heaven above,
Songs rise from the morning haze.

As the day goes on, each stanza of song,
Grows in beauty as we pray.
Lifted to God, our songs of love,
Extend to those we meet each day.

Lift your song to the sky; it is Christ who died,
That we might sing, worship and play.
Again He lives in those who He gives,
Life in Him day after day.

To live this life we can avoid strife,
By turning to Christ in our need.
The clouds once seen take on heavenly sheen,
When our songs shine through our words and deeds.

An old year ends, a new one begins,
Similar to the start of each day.
Raise voices high, and music to the sky,
Our God gives life to who he may.

God sent His Christ to bring you new life,
In each heart that turns to His truth.
The truth of His word will again be heard,
When its music sets glad tongues loose.

Turn your hearts to God while walking this sod,
And sounds of joy will fill your heart.
All joy from Him is free from sin,
Songs of life never to depart.

Matthew 12:34 *"... the mouth speaks out of that which fills the heart.*

75

84 God Rules

Law and order rule the day,
When we rise up and say;
"Glory to God in the highest,"
Reign in my heart today.

Though we seek other kings or guides,
Our God rules only when we abide,
By all that He does when we say,
"Glory to God in the highest,"
Rule in our lives today.

When mankind lets us down,
Look to God whose love abounds.
Declare and sing with hearts uplifted,
"Glory to God in the highest,"
Abide with us as we pray.

When our God hears with His love,
We praise His rule above.
Singing loudly from glad hearts each day,
"Glory to God in the highest,"
Rule in our Land to stay.

Exodus 20:2–3 *...You shall have no other gods before Me.*

85 The Songster

There is a man I know,
Who sings wherever he goes.
His song arises to God on high,
Like a bird fluttering before His eyes.

His limericks don't always rhyme,
Though his words are often sublime.
He sings to our God and Christ our King,
Standing tall in praise each time he sings.

My friend is now growing old,
Yet his music still remains bold.
In most men's eyes he appears almost small,
But in God he still stands tall.

With Christ this man still sings,
In harmony with the King of Kings.
In Christ alone we stand or fall,
In His kingdom none are small,

Psalms 146:2 *I will praise the LORD while I live; I will sing praises to my God while I have my being.*

86 There is a God in Nature
Music: "He Lives" by Alfred H. Ackley 1887-
1960, copyright 1933, 1961 Rodeheaver Co.

There is a God in nature who wants us to obey,
He rises above the tumult when by His words we stay.
His words alone don't save us it takes a state of mind,
Believing Him most wholly with hearts and souls refined.

Refrain
Redeemed, redeemed, our hearts do rise above,
The most majestic mountains, by His unending love
Redeemed, redeemed, this life does shout for joy,
From wooded hills and valleys, His music we deploy.

We look to Him in honor His edicts we obey,
He appears in fields with flowers His love is here to stay.
Those around us blooming with words of hope and praise,
His love seems to surround us His nature is displayed.

The end is the beginning; it's hard to understand,
Our Christ alone exalts us by His unwavering hand.
To realms of peace and glory His love we do enjoy,
Alive with Him forever by fields and streams His choice.

It is to God our glory we give in solemn praise,
His realm seems to surround us since our youngest days.
His mercy is forever to all who He does choose,
To live with Him in gardens that we can never lose.

Romans 1:20 *For since the creation of the world His invisible attributes, His eternal power and divine nature, have been clearly seen, being understood through what has been made, so that they are without excuse.*

CELEBRATIONS

87 One-One-Twenty-One-One   New Year, 1/1/2011

This day has begun; it is One-One-Twenty-One-One,
Can you see the sky, have you seen the Son?
On earth long ago His reign's first begun,
One man, one Son, God man three in one.

He was born; He died, and rose to the skies,
Dead, buried, restored before our very eyes.
Rising again, forgetting our past,
Living with Him, we're alive at last.

Where do we find this Man of renown?
Look in God's word, you'll find there He's shown.
Two millenniums ago His day just began,
His live relived each year, in the hearts of man.

One God, one Son, for heaven He's won,
Each member from earth, singly one by one.
Lives are redeemed by God's only Son,
Again, on this new day, One-One-Twenty-One-One.

Romans 6:4 *Therefore we have been buried with Him through baptism into death, so that as Christ was raised from the dead through the glory of the Father, so we too might walk in newness of life.*

88 Hope for the Future   New Year

The New Year is upon us;
For better or worse.
Do not rely on this,
But on our Savior's birth.

Bearing gifts to those on earth,
Living water to all who thirst.
The gifts He gives are fresh and free,
For those reborn eternally.

We now live spiritually to give,
Encouragement to all who live.
Depressed at times in mind and soul,
Give Him our cares out of control.

Lift up the storms from deep within,
Our Savior then takes hold.
He carries away sins by His Spirit's wind,
Far removed from this world we know.

John 3:8 *The wind blows where it wishes and you hear the sound of it, but do not know where it comes from and where it is going; so is everyone who is born of the Spirit.*

89 Happy Easter   **Easter**

Sunrise gilds the skies,
I see it in your eyes.
It is a given, the Son has risen,
Nevermore to die.

He rose again to give,
Our lives for Him to live.
Living with Him in glory is the age-old story,
Etched on the hearts of all who are His.

We begin anew our life with You
Living words of His through what we do.
A gift from God while we walk this earth,
Proclaiming, "He is risen!" through lives rebirthed.

The Lord is risen on high,
To return one day from the skies.
Watch His life shine from time to time
In the eyes of those who see by His design.

Matthew 13:16 *But blessed are your eyes, because they see; and your ears, because they hear.*

90 Spring   **Easter**

Spring came into my house today,
Palm Sunday has its special way.
Yes, God's glory soon will unfold,
Full of Easter promises of old.

Brought on His wings as in a storm,
God's ways are not this world's norm.
A cloud for one is a blessing for another,
As we treat each other as sisters and brothers.

We all have our own special niche,
Created by God we each exist.
God's love extends to hearths and homes.
His ways exist from when we were born.

His love for one may seem to abound,
While in another He can't be found.
But in reality He is close to each,
Guided by His love to care and teach.

His love appears to come and go,
A rainbow living within my soul.
All of God's promises are here to stay,
Written in the Bible to this day.

John 12:12–13 *...Hosanna! Blessed is He who comes in the name of the Lord, even the King of Israel.*

91 The Day After Easter   Easter

The day after Easter, life has just begun,
The Easter children have all had their fun.
Easter is for grownups, not little ones alone,
The joy of the resurrection will carry us truly home.

Though Easter egg hunts may take their toll,
When little children go out of control.
Candy and eggs behind each tree and bush,
A sugar high for kids, for parents a push.

Pushed into another week just begun,
Parents are smiling under Easter sun.
Kids are more seriously back in school,
For gone is the day when the sugar fairy ruled.

Kids may lack the meaning of the day,
Parents must tell them teaching the way.
Jesus alone rose from the dead,
Freeing our lives from all dreads.

Let us kids on Easter say,
Candy and cake is not the way.
Jesus arose for us all to sing,
Praises to Christ our King.

Mark 16:6 *And he said to them, "Do not be
amazed; you are looking for Jesus the Nazarene,
who has been crucified. He has risen; He is not here....*

92 A Father's Day Lament   Father's Day

My father's gone but he left me a song,
Which told me to cry no longer.
God said to me, "You do belong,
I will satisfy your heartfelt hunger."

"You hungered and thirst for man's love at first,
But now it's My love you must rely on.
Your life here on earth was given at birth,
Heaven and family rejoiced in My song."

"The joy in your life was not without strife,
This is meant for you to grow on.
Sadness becomes delight when from within your life,
You depend on My word to survive on."

Psalms 119:105 *Your (God's) word is a lamp
to my feet and a light to my path.*

93 Anniversaries   **Anniversaries**

Most anniversaries are joyous, though some are sad,
Others are about trouble, most make us glad.
Time spent reminiscing does not waste the day,
Sadness and glad thoughts are here to stay.

Glad thoughts refresh better days gone before,
Anniversaries of hard times open future doors.
Remembering travesties strengthens freedoms call,
Those early days when we no longer crawled.

Glad thoughts are subtly brought into mind,
When times of great joy are pleasantly assigned.
Rejoicing together in a multitude of friends,
Brings back happy days as they first began.

Gladness and sadness from the depths of our hearts,
Makes each anniversary a brand new start.
One brings sheer joy while the other tends to blind,
Good things to be remembered, the bad left behind.

Proverbs 10:7 *The memory of the*
righteous is blessed...

94 Wedding Day   **Marriage**

Marriage is bliss, when lived for one another,
Heavenly kisses, from sisters and brothers.
Our God is faithful to those whom He loves,
Marriages on earth are formed high above.

To have and to hold, together for life,
Does not circumvent testings of strife.
To hug and make up is joyful to see,
By God up above who loves both you and me.

Mark 10:6–8 *Jesus said, and the two shall become one flesh; so they are no longer two, but one flesh.*

95 America's 4ᵗʰ of July

4ᵗʰ of July

The fourth stands for forgiveness,
When God set our Nation free.
Not by might or power,
But by His wise mercy.

We stand tall and proud,
In a world encompassed by fear.
Standing together as Americans,
Drying this world's tears.

Anxieties, fears and worries,
Plague many homes today.
But the God of peace listens,
As we humbly bow and pray.

Cast all your cares on our Creator,
Who made everything you see.
He sent His Son into the world,
Extending love and mercy.

All who call on the name of Jesus,
Have peace reign within their hearts.
Though this world may quake around you,
His comforting peace will not depart.

John 8:36 *So if the Son makes you free, you will be free indeed.*

96 Giving Thanks   Thanksgiving

Thanksgiving is a state of heart and mind,
It evades the proud, but blesses the kind.
It begins when you look around and see,
God's love abounds from sea to sea.

It began with Pilgrims and Natives in kind,
Celebrating life in God's new land sublime.
Feasting, games, fellowship and fun,
In joy the first Thanksgiving was begun.

Open your very heart, mind and life,
Welcome hurting souls torn with strife.
Feast, laugh, kid and sing,
It is our Christ who is the King.

Put to rest all dirt from the past,
Celebrate with your full heart at last.
Christ alone is our cornerstone,
His life begins in our hearts, His home.

Built on the Rock this house stands,
Thankful for gifts from God's kind hand.
In harmony this home resounds in joy,
The revelry begins with each girl and boy.

Once begun we easily behold,
The love of God as it unfolds.
Children and adults together release,
Love for each other from sea to sea.

Psalms 107:1 *Oh give thanks to the LORD, for He is good, for His lovingkindness is everlasting.*

97 Plymouth Shores   Thanksgiving

The Pilgrims did bring, to America's kings,
The Lord Jesus Christ in their hearts.
The Lord's Spirit spread, to both living and dead,
By the news Christ's life did depart.

Christ's message remains, today just the same,
As told on Plymouth's shores.
This I see, that He died just for me,
And together our lives are restored.

Lives now released, live here in peace,
In thanksgiving from shore to shore.
Once destined to die, hands rose on high,
In adulation to our Savior and Lord.

It's easy to see, in this Land of the Free,
God's light shining for all to see.
Hearts abound, with majestic sounds,
Of thanksgiving, when Christ sets us free.

John 8:36 *So if the Son makes you free,
you will be free indeed.*

98 Thanksgiving   Thanksgiving

On bended knees we seek Thee,
The God of all creation.
With thankful hearts we make a start,
Singing praises in adoration.

Today we pray, this Thanksgiving Day,
For the providence You've generously given.
It is You we seek in humility,
Rich through acts in Your Son's redemption.

We hold our heads high and do not deny,
The gift of Your Son high in heavens,
Your gift to mankind in lives is defined,
Found peacefully in hearts forgiven.

The Pilgrims abound in this Land of renown,
With Indians You've graciously given,
Freedom in our land by Your command,
Living together in peaceful conditions.

Peace You have given to both Pilgrims and Indians,
To live joyfully together while living.
For each does receive a measure of belief,
Bringing life together, forever forgiven.

Psalms 147:7–9 *Sing to the Lord with thanksgiving...*

99 Christmas Sings   Christmas

Christmas sings through angels; wings,
The sound above is His pure love.
Angels abound with angelic sound,
Heard by ears tuned to God's kingdom above.

Songs arise out of days gone by,
Created by heaven's open doors.
Living on high, music from the skies,
Alive today from what life restores.

Shepherds sing our Savior's name,
Angel wings proclaim the same.
Together the music reaches heaven above,
Returning to God who gives us His love.

We sing praises on Christmas for all to hear,
Hoping on hope, our Lord will draw near.
Christ is alive in us today,
In family and friends with whom we pray.

Luke 2:13–14 *And suddenly there appeared*
with the angel a multitude of the heavenly
host praising God and saying, "Glory to God in the highest,
and on earth peace among men with whom He is pleased."

100 The Gift   Christmas

Truth is conclusive, not elusive,
Where is it found? It's all around.
Look to the heavens, the stars, the sky,
The seas and streams declare the Supreme.

When in doubt all creation shouts,
"God's word thrives! We are alive!"
Look in the Bible, His word is reliable,
His truth is professed by words we confess.

Listen to the lie and you can't deny,
Its joys are fleeting, the results defeating.
Sin destroys things once enjoyed,
Lost to posterity were acts of charity.

The joy of giving is a gift for the living,
God offers us life, a free gift, His delight.
His gift is to give that we might live,
His Son was given to all that are living.

"Peace on earth good will to men!"
Is declared by God on earth again.
Look to our Lord this Christmas time,
His throne is your home when He is thine.

Isaiah 9:6 (KJV) *For unto us a child is born, unto us a son is given: and the government shall be upon his shoulder: and his name shall be called Wonderful, Counselor, the mighty God, the everlasting Father, the Prince of Peace.*

101 Peace, Goodwill on Earth   Christmas

Jesus died, was crucified,
A tragedy for His chosen.
When He arose, the grave foretold,
Into glory that was pre-spoken.

Christ was born, the world mourned,
Its sinful ways are ended.
The King arose in swaddling clothes,
In the form that God intended.

His birth was heralded by angels,
While shepherds resounded with joy.
His death was directed by Satan's throng,
While heavenly witnesses were deployed.

Born on this earth for the second birthed,
Our joy is now expanded.
Our God reigns through His Son;
Satan's world has been upended.

Get on your knees all who see,
The wonders of Christ's birth.
This Christmas time is now assigned,
For peace, goodwill on earth.

Luke 2:29–32 *A Light of revelation to the Gentiles, and the glory of Your people Israel.*

PEOPLE

102 Alone   **Friends**

A day in one's life is unlike another's,
Each life is separate from sisters and brothers.
Surrounded by friends never to depart,
Is the goal of many said from the start.

The truth is life continues on,
When even our best friends are suddenly gone.
We stand alone, even within a crowd,
When Life crashes down in a demeaning shroud.

Life continues on in hearts and minds,
Tendered by God through your life in time.
Nearness is separated in our lives so lived,
Temporarily parted by our God who forgives.

Each of us shall return one day,
To the Creator of life with Him to stay.
Friends will be seen in a new light,
Changed by our God in whom we delight.

Standing tall before His throne,
Reaping rewards gained through Him alone.
For only Christ sustains by grace,
Bringing us together to a heavenly place.

Matthew 28:20 *Jesus said, "Lo, I am with you always, even to the end of the age."*

103 Peacemakers   Friends

Peacemakers are a blessing, for God gives them light.
Making life's deep, darkness shine with heavenly light.

To the farthest recesses of our mind,
God's peace is extended to all mankind.

Shining from the midst of hurt, pain and sorrow;
The peace of God gives bright hope for tomorrow.

When dawn appears in glory, splendor and light;
Our hearts are lifted from the darkest of nights.

The peace of God transcends hearts and minds;
Like bands of gold on those peacefully inclined.

Healing hands fuse broken hearts, minds and souls;
As the peacemaker restores lives to have and to hold.

Matthew 5:9 *Blessed are the peacemakers, for they shall be called sons, and daughters, of God.*

104 Together We Stand   **Friends**

Fellowship is the key, I've found,
Meeting with men from town to town.
Fellowship demands each one to be,
Guided by God for all to see.

When in His hand we all understand,
Each one's desire within these bands.
Bands of wisdom, bands of love,
Bands that bind us with Him above.

Men can be men, this I see,
Perched on the edge of eternity.
Fears and doubts wash away,
When men gather together to ask and pray.

Men are strongest when they seek,
Help from each other their souls to keep.
Men stand tallest in this life,
When they gather together beyond common strife.

Gathered in Him men stand firm,
Against the foes of life determined.
Doctors, lawyers, priests and kings,
When working together make hearts sing.

Men gathered in unity stand,
Tallest when living in a free land.
Standing together for all to see,
That none act independently.

When in the eyes of God we're seen,
Unified in Christ's blood we're clean.
Cleansed to march forth on earth once again,
Fighting and warring against lust, greed and sin.

2 Timothy 4:7 *I have fought the good fight, I have finished the course, I have kept the faith*

105 Friends at Heart Friends

Friends are gifts to be discerned,
Blessed ones who in God we learn,
Built through devotion, love and care,
Given by God who with us shares.

Friends don't measure, test or tell,
All secret things that we reveal.
Seen in hopes and dreams of the mind,
Given by God to all who are blind.

God restores sight making blind to see,
With new eyes that see His mysteries.
Mysteries hidden in hearts, minds and souls,
Revealed by friends under God's control.

Now we see all those gathered around,
In God's kingdom, friends we have found.
Who love us in spite of who we are,
Like God, friend's love from the heart.

Proverbs 18:24 *A man of too many friends comes to ruin, but there is a friend who sticks closer than a brother.*

106 Subservient Servants Servants

Servants are subservient to those who are blind,
They work in God's light before all of mankind.
The blind who see cannot comprehend,
What for us is beginning, to them is the end.

Our work begins in the light of the Lamb,
Guiding even our blind with His righteous right hand.
The stars are our map as they sing in the heavens,
Glorifying God beyond human comprehension.

Music arises from the children of earth,
Who draw their strength from heaven's rebirth.
Reborn to praise God, our high priest and king,
Christ who arose to make our hearts sing.

Through Christ alone our songs rise to the skies,
A bountiful life for those who on Him rely.
Life given by Him filled with love, joy and peace,
Granted to all as their sin is released.

Though riches and fame may not be ours to hold,
God's bounty is enough, to none He withholds.
He feeds and clothes all He holds in His hands,
In this life, or the next, His chosen ones stand.

To serve is the key to God's bountiful life,
He wipes away tears caused by this world's strife.
Washed clean of world's trials, troubles and woes,
Our God reigns in hearts trustworthy and bold.

Psalms 127:1 *Unless the LORD builds the
house, they labor in vain who build it*

107 Day Without End   **Servants**

One day ends where another begins,
Nighttime arrives, but is not the end.
Darkness and light are ethereal in this life,
The difference astounds even my wife.

CHIMES

The end of night and breaking of dawn,
Does not always bring a fulfilling song.
A crabby man in dawn's early light,
Doesn't normally continue to night.

Coffee, tea and milk does nourish,
Early morning joy to flourish.
Hauling garbage, cleaning pans,
Restores harmony in this house again.

Cut the grass, trim the shrubs,
Scrubbing floors remove any crud.
Cluttered house and cluttered minds,
Go hand in hand, much of the time.

The yard is neat, the house is clean,
My mind is straight again, it seems.
A good book ends when darkness begins,
Back to bed, to resume all over again.

Ecclesiastes 2:22–23 *For what does a man get in all his labor and in his striving with which he labors under the sun?*

108 Nursery School   Teachers

School is for kids, I've often been told,
It's not for adults that are growing old.
We quake and quiver when called to recite,
While youth, on the other hand, consider it delight.

When classes begin, simple and serene,
The minds of the youth appear fresh and clean.
As the student gets older much clutter is there,
Aging minds show lives marked by worries and cares.

Grandiose dreams of imagination flare,
From the lips of the young with nary a care.
Dreams bruised and broken fill the hearts of the aged,
Revived by God's wisdom in these ancient sages.

Up peaks and down valleys we travel together,
The young and the old united forever.
Praise God alone, the exalted, enthroned,
He gathers together all He brings home.

Hebrews 11:16 ...*God is not ashamed to be*
called their God; for He has prepared a city
for them.

109 The Bruised Reed   Teachers

Bruised reeds are essential to life,
Those who break them experience strife.
But those who heal them are beyond compare,
Akin to our Savior, faithfully there.

Though physical and mental anguish destroy us,
Thank God for those who heal and restore us.
Whether doctors, nurses, pastors or priests,
Their place in this world is one to teach.

Their job is paramount to all things around us,
Through them the love of Christ astounds us.
Place us on track, repaired and together,
Together proceeding forward forever.

Restored and strengthened we walk on this sod,
Giving praise and thanks to our loving God.
We thank Him for gifts of healing in love,
Sent to this world from His kingdom above.

Isaiah 42:3 *A bruised reed He will not break and a dimly burning wick He will not extinguish...*

110 Ministry   Ministers

Ministers may live a life, free of fear, trouble and strife,
Though maybe true for others, this doesn't ring true for me.
Trouble and strife seems to abound, unless fully in God
    we're found,
But we learn to perceive, God's love still thrives in
    difficulties.

Anyone worth his salt, believes things eventually turn out,
Life fills with trials, troubles and joy, experienced by all
    whom God deploys.
Enjoy each part of this life while you can, it's His rich grace
    given to all of His men.
Though grace is often slowly perceived by those in whom
    it's been received.

Love for life is a mystery, which in God's realm the blind do
    see.
Blind as bats we wander around often seen as the town's
    clown.
It's hard to comprehend how our lives correct sin.
Perhaps someday we'll be told, what God fully accomplished as
    lives unfold.

Now I live just to see, what each day God has waiting for me.
Living one day at a time, giving love and hope to all
    mankind.
The biggest lesson we must still learn, is humility before our
    works do burn.
Before our God we all will stand, presenting lessons learned
    by His hand.

Psalms 104:4 *He makes the winds His messengers, flaming fire His ministers.*

111 An Ode to a Minister and Friend
Ministers

Birthdays come and go, but this one thing I know,
The word of our Lord goes on forever.

Those who teach and preach find strength at Jesus's feet,
Taught by our Lord and Savior.

Jesus will teach those who seek His word from above, given
in love,
By men of faith seeking God's face,
Found full of grace in the Bible.

When in turn we do return, to God singing praise and adoration,
Brought by men of God who walk this sod,
Proclaiming God's grace and wisdom.

We stand in awe before our God,
While teaching His word at home and abroad,
Gained by diligently, searching His Holy Scripture.

When by His hand we finally stand, before God's throne in
Heaven,
He will reward those who adore, his word entrusted to man
forever.

Confidently go forth from man to man, spreading the Gospel
throughout the land,
The day will come when our work is done, but our years will
continue forever.

Psalms 119:105 *Your word is a lamp to my feet and a light to my path.*

112 Little by Little   Craftsmen

Little by little God's hand does whittle,
Gone are life's chips in our way.
The person thus formed within God's storm,
Lives to see the break of new days.

God's love wielded from above,
As a mallet breaks waste away.
The chips in our life are burdens and strife,
That prevent us from greeting each day.

The chips, once they're gone, enable each son,
To successfully walk in God's way.
Gone from this life are the sins causing strife,
As God, through His Son, takes them away.

God's love for man, we can't comprehend,
Until our sins are cast far away.
What remains we can see is you and me,
Created by God as we pray.

2 Corinthians 5:17 *Therefore if anyone is
in Christ, he is a new creature; the old
things passed away; behold, new things
have come.*

113 Soldiers Brave and Free   Soldiers

The brave and the free standing side by side,
They both stood for love yet both of them died.
Bravely together they fought the good fight,
One fought to the death, the other found life.

One fought on earth his soil to defend,
Fighting for freedom, for family and friends.
He sought to restore freedom on earth,
Once lost to the enemy of God's rebirth.

The other fought in heavenly realms up above,
The specter of a Nation's death, his motive for love.
He fought for life's principles we cannot see,
To regain all lives, precious, and free.

Both of these men fought the hardness of life,
Dying for freedom on darkest of nights.
Now free to live their lives together in peace,
For God and Country all bondage released.

Philippians 1:21 *For to me, to live is Christ and to die is gain.*

114 Still Valentines
A Good Wife

Through trouble and strife, I still love my wife,
When the pain is gone memories linger on.
It becomes hard to see why she loves me,
Through the darkness of life she is my delight.

Yet, I truly see that she really loves me,
In spite of my faults, I now have no doubts.
It's God's love we see while on bended knees,
Bowing before God for the other's needs.

To love one another is Christ's decree,
Ordered on high from eternity.
It is easy to do when one finally sees,
The love God has placed in thee, to me.

In loving you back, I'm readily pleased,
By memories pleasant, because you love me.
My love in return forever endures,
Because God's love implanted is holy and pure.

Ephesians 5:25–26 *Husbands, love your
wives, just as Christ also loved the church
and gave Himself up for her...*

115 My Wife and Mother of Her Kind   A Good Wife

I have a wife who has endured much strife,
At the hands of her fellow man.
When I was burdened from guilt and sin,
To her arms I fled and she let me in.

Many a child she raised alone at home,
With a breaking heart burdened for her own.
Her children reflect her love in time,
Nurtured by her heart tendered by God's love and mine.

A loving mother and wife shall not be disregarded,
It's evidence of God's work in the kindhearted.
She loved us fully beyond comprehension,
By maternal caring for this world's children.

I return again from this world's strife,
To rest once more in the arms of my wife.
A loving wife and mother who all of us cherish,
May God's love uphold her lest any of us perish.

Proverbs 31:10–12 *An excellent wife, who can find?*

116 God's Delight; a Good Wife   A Good Wife

The sun does shine once again,
Deep within the hearts of men.
They begin to see light with each new day,
When through the Savior they faithfully pray.

Christ hides deep within their hearts,
Released by prayer; an excellent start.
Turning away from our sin,
Is the very best way to begin.

Released and cleansed by Christ's own blood,
Opens our hearts unto the flood.
Peace floods fully through our souls,
When the joy of the Lord's in full control.

Minds fully strained by the acts of men,
Are filtered by love again and again.
Love blooms in each man's fertile life,
Upon the assistance of his good wife.

Wives, in God's light, cause love to grow,
Within mankind's most hardened souls.
The light of God shines most bright,
When magnified through a God-given wife.

Proverbs 31:30 *Charm is deceitful and beauty is vain, But a woman who fears the LORD, she shall be praised.*

117 The Tie That Binds   A Good Wife

Storms of life between husband and wife,
Occur in this world we live in.
They will not depart until our hearts,
Are perfected in love from within.

Hearts in tune with God's Son resume,
To abide together harmoniously.
Apart from Christ we are ostracized,
To live our lives unsuccessfully.

Together we stand in the marriage band,
With Christ, the tie that binds.
I don't understand just how He commands,
Two lives to unite and combine.

Our flesh is weak but is released,
As eagles to soar together.
Until the Son unites us as one,
To love and cherish each other.

Ephesians 5:28, 31, 33 *For this reason a man shall leave his father and mother and shall be joined to his wife, and the two shall become one flesh...*

118 Showers of Love   A Good Wife

Love is given by God to all living,
To seek and to save the lost.
It begins at home when we're alone,
Without wife, cat or dog.

To live alone is hard to condone,
When at the door shall knock.
The one you love and are thinking of,
The true owner of you, the cat and dog.

From God is given the love of living,
To your spouse to share with all.
It came with a price, of great sacrifice,
Christ's life, for your wife, you, cat and dog.

To deny the Christ in the life of your wife,
Is not to see beyond the wall.
As your wife lives, your God richly gives,
Love, life and grace to you, cat and dog.

So begin anew if your actions are true,
In all that you see and find to do.
To bring love and light to the one in your life,
That you love and cherish as your dear wife.

She stands by your side having never denied,
Her love for your God upon whom you've relied.
She still stands tall within God's halls,
Making a home for you, cat and dog.

Ephesians 5:25–33 *Nevertheless, each*
individual among you also is to love his own
wife even as himself...

119 Polished Stones   **A Good Wife**

I have a wife at home,
Who belongs to God alone.
She and I alive as one,
Living together with God under this sun,

With God's help we both stand tall,
Though alone we sometimes fall.
And fall we do from time to time,
Picked up again since God is kind.

God, for a time, may allow us to wander;
Showing mercy when our lives we squander.
Put back on track we travel on,
Guided by the hand of God's own Son.

In Christ alone we venture forth,
Boldly aiding others off course.
Seeking them to give them help,
Saving them from their own selves.

Pulled out free from under our sins,
We now can see deeply within.
Within the hearts of all mankind,
Finding tarnished gold to be refined.

Christ alone has the solution,
For lives stained by this world's pollution.
Cleansed by His holy word alone,
Polished in His hand like precious stones.

1 Peter 2:4–5 *...you also, as living stones, are being built up as a spiritual house for a holy priesthood ...*

120 My Wife, My Life   A Good Wife

Within my heart burns, God's releases from sin,
It spreads through my being erupting from within.
When exposed to the world, God's healing work begins,
It is God who restores the soul so my heart beats again.

Restored to live in Christ, my mission just begins,
To live again for someone else, even my own kin,
Bringing health and life to these old bones hidden beneath
my skin,
My life's my wife, to love and hold; I'm energized again.

Ephesians 5:28 *So husbands ought also to love their own wives as their own bodies. He who loves his own wife loves himself*

HOPE

Start Up

121 Courage

Courage is deceptive,
It comes and it goes,
Courage is contagious,
Neither bought or sold.

Courage is given,
To all of us living.
To either stand tall,
Or be destined to fall.

When once we do stand,
We start over again.
In life it's not over,
Until covered with clover.

When the final die is cast,
Christ's acts alone will last.
To God be the glory,
Is our eternal story.

Galatians 2:20 ... *and the life which I now live in the flesh I live by faith in the Son of God* ...

122 Inspired to Serve

Saved to serve is our battle cry,
No one alive has a dry eye.
Bound for His glory unto the skies,
No eye has seen the waiting surprise.

Called to a destiny free from sin,
The door is wide open to all entering in.
We come and we go wherever we're told,
Guided by His light from days of old.

The life of Christ shines from hearts that unfold,
Cleansed by His nature more precious than gold.
Drawn to redeem the lives of lost men,
When we seem to have finished we begin again.

Life does not end when evils arise,
Lift up your eyes and see paradise.
When times seem black, muddied and bleak,
Our God reigns, His edicts run deep.

Look in your heart and you will see,
A new life destined eternally.
Lives lived for Christ our Godhead bestows,
Inspiration alive for all to behold.

2 Timothy 3:15–17 *All Scripture is inspired by God and profitable for teaching, for reproof, for correction, for training in righteousness*

123 Start, Stop, Restart

Beginning again is the way of men,
Start, stop, and restart, as a result of sin.
Time is of essence, more precious than gold,
Over and over our zeal we withhold.

Into the basement, into the dark,
Into the recesses of our heart.
What we find is hard to reveal,
We cry, we laugh over what we've concealed.

It's often funny to find what we've hidden,
Things very minor have kept us in prison.
Revealed by God's light it's plain to see,
What undermined me is not really me.

It was sin in me clearly plain from the start,
And not the result of a faulty heart.
God's atonement is always free,
By God's love Christ is releasing me.

John 8:36 *So if the Son makes you free, you will be free indeed.*

124 Dearly Kindhearted

When you get old and days seem cold,
Lift your eyes to the skies God created.
It is God alone seated on His throne,
Warming your heart reinstated.

When living alone within your home,
Surrounded by pains all around you.
Do not lose heart, they will not depart,
Before you're redeemed in ways to astound you.

When in the dark you receive a new start,
Through prayer and sound petitions.
On their behalf you begin to cast
Off burdens, cares and conditions.

When once restored you'll never be bored,
In praising God for redemption.
When spouse and friends begin entering in,
As heaven's doors open before them.

Psalms 126:5–6 *Those who sow in tears shall reap with joyful shouting...*

125 Begin

In the beginning; just begin,
When surrounded by your friends.
It's never too late to start anew,
Leading your most courageous crew.

The heart is evil; so I'm told,
But when first created it was bold.
Don't be afraid when looking in,
Beneath the surface of your skin.

A heart tendered by God's love,
Is finely tuned by Him above.
Angels rejoice each step of the way,
Looking forward to His full day.

Each one is rewarded for their good,
While those excluded wish they could.
We try again from beginning to end,
In hope of praise from heaven's friends.

Luke 15:10 *Jesus said, "...I tell you, there is joy in the presence of the angels of God over one sinner who repents."*

Help

126 Eyes Dark and Dreary

When the mind's eye is dark and dreary,
And the sun doesn't seem to shine,
When even your walk is heavy and weary,
It's time to stretch out in time.

Look unto the Creator of everything,
Even if you think you were left behind,
Now rejoice in the Lord who made thee.
Wove you physically after your kind.

A created light show of heavenly beings,
Reflected in hearts loving and kind,
Revealed by our God in things that we dream,
His loving light brings sight to the blind.

Sunshine bounces in waves and beams,
Bringing joy to fainting hearts.
The darkest night is soon redeemed,
When in God's light we take part.

John 8:12 *Then Jesus again spoke to them,
saying, "I am the Light of the world; he who follows
Me will not walk in the darkness, but will have the
Light of life."*

127 Standing Together

Storms abound around us,
And death may appear at every hand.
The storms of life astound us,
Yet we're held firmly in His hand.

Peace always seems elusive,
Where can it be found?
Look again inside you,
Christ is still around.

Christ alone is the stone,
That which we rely on.
The capstone does not stand alone,
We must not deny Him.

Whether we stand or fall,
Is not our sole decision.
Christ alone gives the call,
While we're still under derision.

When we stand, it's by His hand,
We have nothing to be proud of.
He lifts us up to realms above,
Guided by His words of love.

John 18:9 *to fulfill the word which He (Jesus) spoke, "*
Of those whom You have given Me I lost not one."

128 The Dark Valleys

A day in the life of flesh and bone,
Is eventually fulfilled, if left alone.
Alone your thoughts are guided by God,
Until you see the paths you have trod.

God's hand alone forgives and corrects,
Working His wonders in minds bereft.
Lost to humanity are the young and the old,
When sin is allowed to take its toll.

Gone are the days of pain and deceit,
Once a life has gone to sleep.
A life is restored by Christ alone,
When you bravely go with Him home

Storms of life bring you to the brink,
To the specter of death is what you think.
Yet through the storm there is great light,
Christ alone brings us out of night.

Bear up under what God presents,
Within each life, is the means to repent.
Storms are meant to heal and correct,
God's touch extends to His elect.

Touched by the hardships within the storms,
Life now continues, we're no longer alone.
Guided by God we begin to stand,
Straight and tall by His wonderful hand.

Psalms 23:4 *Even though I walk through the valley of the shadow of death, I fear no evil, for You are with me...*

129 The Front Lines of Sin

Those living on front lines of sin,
Know the battles that rage within.
Sin loses, righteousness reigns,
When hearts tuned to God are maintained.

The battle within each heart does spread,
Raising havoc from head to head.
Our wars with sin are never done,
While we live under this sun.

Yet dawn will break in the deepest night,
Putting our darkest thoughts to flight.
Gone are ghosts that haunted our past,
When we walk with our God at last.

Brought to light, day by day,
All fears of darkness flee away.
Sin is observed for what it is,
A scar on live of those who live.

Gone are the worries that plague each soul,
When our lives are placed under God's control.
Though peace of mind may seem elusive,
God's forgiveness remains conclusive.

Cast into the deep, dark sea,
My sins are forgotten eternally.
When God forgives, all sins are gone,
Despite eerie squawks from the tempter's song.

Romans 4:7–8 *Blessed is the man whose sin the*
Lord will not take into account.

130 Freed to Live

Tired of carrying that sin all around?
Cast upon Him your cares profound.
Patience determines; lives freed of burdens,
Sin is released in time undetermined.

Where does one start? Start with your heart,
Where to begin? Begin with your sin.
Confession is good, cleansed by His blood,
His blood for mine, cleansed over time.

Growing older may make us bolder,
Burdens are lifted, by Him who is gifted.
Jesus alone is the cornerstone,
He lifts from hell hearts who therein dwell.

Lifted to sing, in joy to our King,
King of the Jews is the one I choose.
When He first chose me, I became free,
Free to roam, far beyond my home.

Granted new life, me and my wife,
Freed to give, love to those who live.
Life in the hills, where my wife and I dwell,
We now live in peace, as our time doth decrease.

1 John 4:19 *We love, because He first loved us.*

131 Comfort in Times of Trouble

Comfort is elusive,
When hard times try our hearts,
If we hit the wall while running hard,
Our pain very slowly departs.

The loss of friends and loved ones,
Is part of this life below.
The shock upon our system,
Is unpleasant, this I know.

This part of life is inevitable,
Our spirit survives we're told.
It returns to our Creator,
When our bodies become cold.

Our life is one of confusion,
We don't know which way to go.
But the God of all our comfort,
Understands hearts that grow old.

He calls us home when He's ready,
I know He'll understand.
Our ways are errant from time to time,
But He reaches out to hold our hand.

Call on Christ our Savior,
When you're under deep duress.
He will bring comfort to family and friends,
When He is properly addressed

The book of life, the Bible,
Tells us all that we must know.
About this merciful God of ours,
Whose life and death was foretold.

So don't be afraid to call on Him,
He will be your steadfast friend.
A present help in trouble,
He will not forsake you in the end.

Psalms 46:1–3 *God is our refuge and strength, a*
very present help in trouble…

Despair

132 Exposed

Temptations abound in life that surrounds,
Each one with thoughts all our own.
When in our thought life, we continue in strife,
Beyond control when even reborn.

The end draws near as our vision now clears,
We now see our faults and our sins.
Sins developed in time are really only mine,
Non transferable to others that just began.

Beginning again we constantly swim,
In desperation to right each wrong.
When God's work is begun we join in the fun,
Rejoicing in being carried along.

Embarrassingly red, I'd rather be dead,
Than the spectacle that appears in my eyes.
Sin when exposed embarrasses the most bold,
But is forgiven when to the Lord we cry.

Matthew 9:2 ...*Jesus said to the paralytic, "Take*
courage, son; your sins are forgiven."

133 When Love Abounds

When days are hard to understand,
Look around, you're alive in this land.
The land of promise is where you are,
So make the best of all new starts.

Dreariness lies within your mind,
Not in the hearts of fellow mankind.
Look for the crystalline spark of hope,
Planted at birth beyond our control.

Father, Mother, and our God above,
Planted within us the spark of love.
Love within that blooms and grows,
When friendships abound here below.

Not all we see is pleasant at first,
This typically leads to the second birth.
Sunshine and flowers seem to then abound,
When in our lives, full love is found.

John 15:12 *This is My commandment, that you love*
one another, just as I have loved you.

134 Lifting Burdens

Pain and sorrow may rack our soul,
But bearing burdens is our goal.
Some weights try the most loving hearts,
Others refresh us right from the start.

A burden to one is a blessing to another,
Help often comes from a sister or brother.
A friend in need shall not lightly be regarded,
When help to their heart is gracefully imparted.

Burdens lifted by us or by friends,
Make life easier through days without end.
Days that are dreary when the burden stays ours,
Will turn to lightness when lifted to the stars.

Burdens we lift from others in need,
Quickly become our blessing indeed.
Showers of blessings is what we receive,
From one to another in our time of need.

Galatians 6:2 *Bear one another's burdens, and
thereby fulfill the law of Christ.*

135 A Dedicated Life

Being a man again is to live beyond sin,
At times I fall, but arise to stand tall.
In sorrow and grief I sigh with relief,
Christ lifts from the depths hearts broken and bereft.

Whether I stand or whether I fall is not mine to call,
It is God above who calls us in love.
When called in His name, Christ again reigns,
In the hearts of men Christ lives again.

When Christ is alive our hearts are revived,
I now stand for life in this world of strife.
Just look around you God's love surrounds you,
How can we fail when God's love prevails?

Love does not sin, where new life begins,
I'm beginning to see God's love for me.
Mistakes I have made, their corrections delayed,
Onward I walk doing what I talk.

Turning to Christ, I begin a new life,
I began to live when I learned to forgive.
God's forgiveness extends in love to our friends,
When cleansed by our Lord our lives are restored.

Psalms 32:1 *How blessed is he whose transgression
is forgiven, whose sin is covered!*

Kingdom Gained

136 Storms of Life

Peace and tranquility have their day,
But storms in life push them away.
Our surroundings result in what we sow,
But the storms of life make us grow.

People come and people go,
Leaving behind what they sow.
Left behind are tears and sadness,
While in some hearts is joy and gladness.

Tears shed, calm hurting hearts,
They quiet storms before we part.
Life goes on within raging blasts,
Fully realized once they're past.

When storms arise within our lives,
Turn to God who satisfies.
He bears our burdens through them all,
When He's called upon we all stand tall.

Remember Christ, who calmed the seas,
His love extends to you and me.
He calms the storms within our breast,
In Him we find eternal rest.

Psalms 50:15 *Call upon Me in the day of trouble; I shall rescue you, and you will honor Me.*

137 Game Time

Survival was never just a game,
Life and death are not the same.
When we die life does not end,
One man rises, another descends.

Salvation comes to those who wait,
Upon our Lord to set the date.
Life is renewed when we begin,
To turn our lives away from sin.

Restored to life we now can see,
God's plan for us from eternity.
Plans filled with love, joy and peace,
Granted to each upon our release.

All the others who do descend,
Live without God buried in sin.
Life devoid of love, joy and peace,
Is akin to survival on Godless streets.

Make sure your choice while you still can,
Sins are forgiven by the Son of Man,
A repentant heart is what Christ requires,
You'll abound in love singing in His choir.

Lives are securely held and restored,
When sins are forgiven by God's Son, our Lord.
Give homage to Christ, the honor due His name,
The Godhead too, for their love still sustains.

Isaiah 55:6–7 *Seek the LORD while He may be found; Call upon Him while He is near...*

138 Kingdom Seekers

Seeing to believe is often what we perceive,
But not necessarily so in this life here below.
Magicians and sorcerers plague societies today,
But God's word is permanent and here to stay.

God's word is truth, not a figment of mind,
It will go on forever even when eyes are blind.
Sorceries and magic are just puff as they go,
They are soon forgotten by this world we know.

The best this world offers is figmental at best,
Things we purchase rust and decay to our detest.
God's word is permanent, His kingdom proclaims,
Seek His kingdom on earth, His word loudly exclaims.

God gives His children gifts to touch, love and adore.
His word promises, He opens heaven's doors.
When we live by His word, we reap great reward,
Righteousness is ours forever, in heaven stored.

Matthew 6:33 *Jesus said, "But seek first His kingdom and His righteousness, and all these things will be added to you.*

139 Ann

Pain and sorrow go hand in hand,
Death and darkness rule our land.
Light and life restore each soul,
God's promise is: He's still in control.

Life again will shine and rise,
Lives in God will one day surprise.
Life as we know it blooms and grows,
Lives in God's hand, He beautifully controls.

John 11:25–26 *Jesus said to her... "everyone who lives and believes in Me will never die...."*

140 I am Heading Home and Not Alone

This trial is past, I'm heading home at last,
I am fed, clothed and loved.
All things of this world are left behind,
I am no longer tired, hungry and blind.

The people I know, both here and below,
Are beside me when I pray.
I thank my God day to day,
For all friends with me here today.

1 Corinthians 2:9 *but just as it is written, "Things which eye has not seen and ear has not heard, and which have not entered the heart of man, all that God has prepared for those who love Him."*

REDEMPTION

141 Redemption

The mark of sin upon my brow,
I go through this world alive somehow.
Life is fleeting, life is vain,
But Christ rules in my heart again.

Though tempters continue to rise and fall,
They are defeated when we call.
Call on Christ's name in any despair,
He is God's Son, the one who cares.

He cared enough to calm the seas,
Dying on the cross for you and me.
He died alone for all to see,
Extending mercy to whom He's pleased.

Cast all your sins at His feet,
Leave them behind for all to see.
Strength will then surge within your soul,
When every sin is let go.

Living water from you will flow,
When His love is the center of your soul.
When your love for God is extended,
Expressed by your deeds as God intended.

Psalms 42:5 *Why are you in despair, O my soul? And why have you become disturbed within me? Hope in God, for I shall again praise Him For the help of His presence.*

142 "Everyone Does It!"

"Everyone does it," are not the words,
Bringing forgiveness from our Lord.
"Everyone docs it," is the scourge,
Condemning each with its discord.

Condemning habits are hard to break,
Though sought with tears sincerely made.
Recurring faults our sinful bed we make,
Restored to grace when at Jesus feet they're laid.

"Birds of a feather flock together,"
Are condemning words in many eyes.
But birds together of different feathers,
Make us, "Healthy, wealthy and wise."

Sin perceived is seldom conceived,
When we're walking in the light.
Turning from sin is a sound decree,
Pulling us out of the darkest night.

Returning to God is His delight,
Joy restored to hearts forlorn.
The spirit is won in the fight of the night,
When the cloak of righteousness is worn.

Joel 2:12–14 *...Now return to the LORD your God, for He is gracious and compassionate... Who knows whether He will not turn and relent and leave a blessing behind Him ...?*

143 Peace and Rest

There is a peace I understand,
That rules within the heart of man.
A peace we cannot comprehend,
Because of unforgiven sin.

Sin unquenched often leads
To blindness once conceived.
Blindness in the heart of man,
Eventually spreads from hand to hand.

Spreading out for the world to see,
What God has wrought in the blind who see.
Where sin has spread within the soul,
The grace of God must take control.

Our God one day long ago,
Sent His Son to make us whole.
He quenches the flames of sin again,
When we truly turn to Him.

Peace one day will return to man,
When the blind who see are fully cleansed.
Tarnished hearts will be renewed,
As one by one our Lord does move.

Isaiah 26:3 (KJV) *Thou wilt keep him in perfect peace, whose mind is stayed on thee: because he trusteth in thee.*

144 Winter Storms

Winter Storms come with a fury,
Catching men in a hurry
Winds and waves descend in earnest,
Engulfing men of dreams with purpose.

Purpose driven lives are fine,
When guided by our Lord's own mind.
The mind of Christ lives in His own,
Enabling us to kneel before His throne.

When humility resides within our heart,
God grants peaceful grace as a start.
Tempest tossed waves never cease,
Our hearts must strive for permanent peace.

Worship and praise are the key,
Active in the lives of those who believe.
Go alone to God through Christ,
He will calm the storms of life.

When peace resides within our soul,
Thank God for making it so.
Turn your life around to please,
The one whose hands hold eternity;

God's word alone shall be our guide,
It has full power to satisfy.
Storm after storm, life continues on,
Peace is elusive to the weak and the strong.

God helps those living their lives for Him,
Who have stopped striving after wind.
When living life by God's holy word,
Artful tack through storms is secured.

Matthew 7:13–14 *Jesus said, "Enter through the narrow
gate; for the gate is wide and the way is broad that leads to
destruction, and there are many who enter through it. For
the gate is small and the way is narrow that l
eads to life, and there are few who find it.*

145 Trusting

Trust in God and you will see,
In this He is well pleased.
Walk alone and you can tell,
Without God, the path leads to hell.

When we walk alone by sight,
Absent from God's revealing light.
Our path is clouded, dreary and hard,
Full of remorse from the start.

Abel's brother, Cain, could not withstand,
A remorseful heart brought on by his own hand.
God's merciful act released from death,
The judgment Cain earned by stopping breath.

God released Cain for all to see,
How He extends sinners His mercy.
On Cain's brow God put a mark,
Sparing his life from vengeful hearts.

No longer could Cain sow and reap,
The land that once furnished his keep.
Cain then went into the land of Nod,
Building cities instead of breaking sod.

CHIMES

We in the fallen human race,
Likewise experience God's grace.
Through His obedience on the cross,
Christ redeeming us who were lost.

Christ rose again for the world to see,
The pathway reaching eternity.
Life with Him will forever be,
Alive with joy, love and peace.

Genesis 4:15 *So the Lord said to him, "Therefore whoever kills Cain, vengeance will be taken on him sevenfold." And the Lord appointed a sign for Cain, so that no one finding him would slay him.*

146 Corinthians Today

If the Corinthians retained proper hearts and minds,
They would not be in trouble so much of the time.
Yet their minds then are like ours today,
Just look around you, hear what people say.

The Corinthians had a good heart to start,
But inner troubles tore them apart.
Bickering, badgering, struggles to be supreme,
Taking its toll, making their appearance mean.

Many of us have not yet learned,
The art of compassion is God's concern.
God's work on our hearts has just begun,
If He has caught us while we are still young.

Young at heart, so easy to sway,
We, like the Corinthians, could easily say;
"We want to go our own way!"
Thank God, on the other hand, He's with us to stay.

Take heart young church in the land of Nod,
God does not sleep, but lives on this sod.
His hand still strengthen, supports and corrects,
Those standing tall in His righteousness.

"Rise and shine!" the earth resounds,
When the joy of growth in our land is found.
Growth in humility and purpose to live,
Is found in each other when God forgives.

Luke 20:21 *They questioned Him, saying, "Teacher, we know that You speak and teach correctly, and You are not partial to any, but teach the way of God in truth.*

147 Deep Needs

What do you need? "A piece of bread please."
What did you get? "Deeper in debt."
Where did you go? "To a banker I don't know."
What did he give? "Nothing to live."

Where should you start? "Look for a new heart."
Where is this found? "Far above ground."
What is the price? "God's kingdom is right."
What do I pay? "God's Son paid the way."

How do I know which way to go?
"Look up and live, God's Son fully forgives."
What will I find? "God's love is kind."
Where do I begin? "Repent of your sins."

How is this done? "On your knees to God's Son."
What do I say? "Forgive me each day."
What's God's call? "Forgiveness to all."
How do I respond? "Praise God in song."

John 5:22–23 *For not even the Father judges anyone, but He has given all judgment to the Son…*

148 All Things Become New

There is a moment in the day that rings joy every way,
Joy arises within the soul when our God's in control.
Ruled by love, not fear or hate, God leads in this debate.
Joy returns to lives conformed by His wise leading of those
reformed.
We are reborn when in our lives God's light shines through
to paradise.
A paradise not seen by man, but residing in hearts of those
once condemned.
Condemned to die we now arise because of Christ once cru-
cified.
Because He died and rose again, we now stand pardoned,
uncondemned.
Freed from the sins entangling our souls since Christ came in
to regain control.

Let the eyes of all who see behold God's love from sea to sea.
This land of ours will return again within the grasp of Christ
our king.
Regaining strength in love and life we will flee all unholy
strife.
We'll rise instead keeping in tune with Christ our king re-
turned to rule.
Ruling in life, death and peace, He rules even those in
eternal sleep.
All will arise in much surprise when we behold Christ in
paradise.
A paradise created by God the Son, the Father and Spirit all
three in one.
United again so all will see the light of God from eternity.
A light destined to restore our lives again to Eden's open door.

1 Thessalonians 4:16–17 *For the Lord Himself will descend from heaven with a shout...and the dead in Christ will rise first. ...and so we shall always be with the Lord.*

149 The Prisoner

A wise man's wisdom begins in the heart,
The fear of God is a good start.
It's ironic to think that a man can begin,
To grow wise as a result of his sin.

Sin when mature leads to death,
But the fear of God leads to righteousness.
Some fear is useful to a healthy mind,
Preventing us from entering into sin and crime.

Laws are made to keep, not be broken,
The laws of God are boldly spoken.
Spoken from the highest mountains and hills,
His Word will never be silenced or quelled.

His word resounds through hearts and minds,
Never seen, but firmly in man designed.
The voice of our conscience controls,
The actions of each man's body and soul.

Left to run wild and amuck,
The thoughts of man are like a garbage truck.
Loaded with daily trash and debris,
Destined for dark eternity.

But once we let God's light shine in,
It reveals the consequences of sin.
God's word will soon become our delight,
Transforming every darkness into light.

Job 28:28 *And to man He said, 'Behold, the fear of the Lord, that is wisdom; and to depart from evil is understanding.'*

150 Heaven on Earth

Be strong in the Lord, we hear the cry,
Lift up your eyes, He will not be denied.
He came to earth, suffered and died,
That we might live in paradise.

We live for Christ; not dying in vain,
We'll live again, our lives regained.
Forever we'll live in realms above,
Restored to health and joy in love.

Our lives on earth too soon do end,
But then in Christ we'll live again.
Yet don't take life on earth too light,
Time spent here is great delight.

When lived for Christ our days ascend,
Unto the stars where they began.
The star, our sun, shines on each face,
Making room for each created race.

Luke 17:20–21 *Jesus said, ... "The kingdom of God is not coming with signs to be observed; ... For behold, the kingdom of God is in you.*

EPILOGUE

To God be the glory,
Is the theme of this story.
There are no bragging rights,
In God's kingdom of light.

His gifts are freely given,
Through His Spirit living.
To build, encourage and unite
The earthly Church is His delight.

1 Thessalonians 5:11 *Therefore encourage one another and build up one another, just as you also are doing.*

Our marching orders are to build up the Church and encourage one another. That is my hope and desire in offering this volume of poetry growing from my lifetime of loving God's word.

Pastors or teachers, preaching the Bible, learn to cope with the experience of going through the valleys of the shadow of death in preparing sermons for congregations or counseling. They understand that if the material doesn't convict him or her while being prepared, it will do little for its recipients.

Writing Godly poetry from a biblical perspective, parallels the role of a pastor or teacher. Here the emotional impact on the author arises from facing the valley of the shadow and having God's spirit lift the writer, and hopefully the reader, to new heights in God's Kingdom of light.

My poems are sometimes rooted and grounded in joy, sometimes laughter, but more frequently, like many of David's Psalms, from feelings of struggle or inadequacy. These feelings are alleviated as God frees from the valley of the shadow of death between the time where the poem begins and its conclusion.

May the poems contained in *Spirit Winds with Chimes* cleanse, refresh, bring you hope, and strengthen your faith.

SPIRIT WINDS WITH CHIMES
Poems Alphabetized by title

SPIRIT WINDS WITH CHIMES
Poems Alphabetized by title

A friend loves at all times.
And a brother is
born for adversity.

-Proverbs 17:17

For me to live is Christ

Dan Wainright